English in a Decade
of Change

English in a Decade of Change

by Michael F. Shugrue

PEGASUS NEW YORK

ACKNOWLEDGMENTS

I should like to express my gratitude to the following individuals and associations: to the American Council on Education for permission to quote from *Improving College Teaching;* to the Association of Departments of English for permission to quote from the *ADE Bulletin;* to Holt, Rinehart and Winston for permission to quote from Herbert J. Muller's *The Uses of English,* Copyright © 1967 by Holt, Rinehart & Winston, Inc.; to the Modern Language Association of America and to the National Council of Teachers of English for permission to quote from a wide variety of their publications; to the National Association of Secondary School Principals for permission to quote from the special issue of the *NASSP Bulletin* devoted to "The English Curriculum in the Secondary School"; to the President and Fellows of Harvard College for permission to quote from Jerome S. Bruner's *The Process of Education;* and to Professors Wallace W. Douglas, Albert H. Kitzhaber, Paul A. Olson, and Erwin R. Steinberg for permission to quote from the curriculum materials prepared by the Curriculum Study Centers in English at Northwestern University, the University of Oregon, the University of Nebraska, and Carnegie-Mellon University.

FOR HELEN AND MARGARET

Contents

Preface

This volume on the teaching and learning of English is a status report on the one school subject required of all students through the twelfth grade and enrolling the greatest number of undergraduates in American colleges and universities. It reviews and assesses a decade of change and innovation in a discipline vital to the intellectual and aesthetic health of a technological, materialistic, impersonal society. It surveys trends in the preparation of teachers of English, the English curriculum at all levels, and patterns of school and college organization which affect the teaching of English from kindergarten through graduate school.

A profession can boast that it flourishes when its members must struggle to keep abreast of an expanding body of significant scholarly and pedagogical research. This boast cannot mask, however, the time lag between the generation of an important theory or teaching technique and its wide adoption in the English classroom. The college professor finds it difficult enough to read the flood of articles, monographs, and books written by those interested in his special field. Because he cannot find time to study new pedagogical ideas and teaching materials with that same scholarly care, he accepts and employs them cautiously, wisely realizing that curriculum innovation needs scrutiny lest it lead to mere faddishness in English studies. The busy classroom teacher, almost always meeting more than 100 pupils a day in five classes and frequently less well prepared as a teacher of English than he needs to be, can incorporate new ideas only when—and if— he has the time to examine new textbooks and to participate in in-service programs and institutes. For all teachers of English, the time lag between theoretical discussions of curriculum in professional journals and books and change in classroom practices grows with the teacher's inability to read widely and regularly enough about change in the teaching of English, to consult with colleagues, and to experiment in his own classroom.

The justification for this book is that it tries to survey what has been achieved in English in the 1960's, to outline new responsibilities for the teacher of English, especially at the college level, and to suggest promising techniques and classroom patterns for the English classroom of the 1970's. The book, addressed first of all to my colleagues in college and university departments of English, provides a general view of English as it is being taught in elementary and secondary schools, junior and community colleges, four-year institutions, and graduate schools. It is not intended, however, merely to provide information about pedagogy for the curious college English teacher, but to suggest directions and activities for college departments of English, to reinforce the responsibilities of college professors of English in teacher preparation programs for elementary and secondary school teachers, and, I hope, to kindle the interest of more college teachers of English in curriculum change in the public schools of the United States as well as in their own college and university departments. It is a sobering thought for any college teacher to recognize that in almost every class he teaches, he is helping to prepare classroom teachers and to stimulate young men and women to enter college teaching. Through his methods, personality, and choice of materials, he both consciously and unconsciously influences the curriculum from first grade through college. His participation in professional meetings encourages wide public support for local, state, and federal research programs, curriculum experimentation, and inservice institutes for teachers of English, as well as promotes articulation among teachers of English at all levels. His awareness of trends in the teaching of English and a greater involvement in the education of school teachers can lead, too, to a reexamination and revitalization of his own teaching. Most college professors of English do not stop often enough to realize how much impact they are already having on American public education—and how much more they could have. Without that realization, many professors fail to look beyond the boundaries of their own campuses. I hope this volume will help to raise their sights.

Because this book is about the English teacher and his subject in schools and colleges, it should prove useful to elementary school teachers and secondary school teachers of English as well as to curriculum coordinators and school administrators. Many classroom teachers who have participated in the conventions, commissions, and committees of the NCTE and in NDEA summer institutes have already been introduced to recent developments in linguistics and rhetoric. Yet even they may be interested in the broad survey of national directions in the development of English which this book attempts. Every educator should finish the volume with more knowledge about trends in and controversies about the teaching of English. The survey

should stimulate English teachers at every level to talk more frequently with one another about their teaching; without such dialogue
on the part of teachers, the profession cannot remain healthy.

The study should interest the educated reader who wishes to learn
about changes in the teaching of English in the last ten years. Such
knowledge will help him understand his responsibilities as a parent
and taxpayer. Bond issues to pay for new buildings, better salaries
for teachers, experimental curriculums, demonstration centers, and
"learning centers"; state aid for research in teaching, statewide television networks, and inservice programs for teachers; and continuing
federal support for education demand an educated, informed, responsive electorate. This volume tries to explain how excellence in
the preparation of English teachers and in the subject matter which
they teach contributes to the intellectual vitality of the school and of
the community and to suggest areas which need additional support.

If a selective and personal study such as this one quickly becomes
outdated, that testifies only to the richness and liveliness of the profession which it describes. Although no review of current thinking
and practice can or should be valid for a decade, it may help later
scholars and teachers to understand the forces which led to curriculum change in the 1960's and to review previous debates, discussions,
studies, and opinions in order to avoid having to repeat them. I have
looked back only as far as the Basic Issues Conferences supported by
the Ford Foundation in 1958 because English has undergone a significant transformation since then. While I have tried not to mis-
represent trends since 1958, to oversimplify what are always compli
cated issues, or to neglect significant achievements of the decade, I
have necessarily had to omit many projects and studies from my survey.
The accumulation of information about English, however, merits a
periodic sorting out such as I have tried to provide in the following
pages, however impressionistic it may finally be. I have not attempted
to write a comprehensive history of the teaching and learning of
English in the United States since Colonial days or to examine even
the most significant studies in English before 1958. The books, articles,
and research reports flowing from the Modern Language Association
and from the National Council of Teachers of English and the richness and variety of the programs at annual and regional meetings of
teachers of English will adequately supplement my sketch and clarify,
for the teacher who wishes to pursue them, issues not raised here.
If this volume helps the English teacher (whether college professor
or classroom teacher in the school), the school and college administrator, and the interested citizen to understand better the changes in
the field of English during a period of phenomenal growth in American education, it will have served its purpose.

My attempts to read about and participate in projects and programs
to improve teacher preparation and the English curriculum and the

increasing difficulty I found in adequately reviewing the books and journals which regularly cross my desk and remembering the alphabet of acronyms which has sprung up in English encouraged me to write this volume now. Talking with teachers in schools and colleges across the United States over the past five years, I have learned that they too were finding it more and more difficult to keep pace with changes in the profession. Seminars with NDEA institute participants from 1965 through 1968 and conversations with graduate students at New York University convinced me that my colleagues and fellow teachers might welcome a synthesis of the changes in English in the 1960's. Five major questions finally determined the contents of this book:

1. What is the nature of English? This is a subject so variously defined, so often discussed, that most English teachers accept automatically the safety of the standard classification into the tripod of language, literature, and composition, even though leading American and British scholars and teachers are emphasizing the centrality of language in the classroom, reasserting the humaneness of the subject, and questioning the emphasis on the content of English which has characterized curriculum development since the Basic Issues Conferences.

2. What is actually being taught in English classrooms around the United States? Because the curriculum reforms of the 1960's have hardly begun to reach most American schools or influence college classrooms, one wonders what is currently being taught under the name of English and how quickly and in what ways change will occur.

3. What developments in literary theory, linguistics, methodology, and technology are likely to affect the teaching of English in the 1970's? Are the innovations in classroom organization and pupil assignment which the newspapers and magazines describe with growing frequency likely to reach the average classroom in the average school? The so-called "linguistics explosion" and the growing acceptance of modular scheduling, residential colleges within multiversities, television, and the computer inevitably have enormous significance for the English classroom.

4. Who is teaching English in the schools and colleges of the United States? As education becomes the major economic and social force in American life, teachers of English, constituting the largest single segment of the 2.6 million teachers in the United States, become a powerful social and intellectual force in the nation. One must ask, especially in the light of recent research reports outlining the deficiencies in his preparation and his—typically heavy—workload, how well prepared the English school teacher is today, how responsive he will be to innovation in the classroom, and what steps are being taken by professional associations and by the federal government to improve the competency of tomorrow's teacher of English. These questions are all the more fascinating because American society awards its greatest

prestige to those committed to technology rather than to the humanities, but demands at the same time the deep involvement and commitment of English teachers to the staggering problems of inner-city schools and disadvantaged youngsters. Because their tasks are so varied, one wonders how teachers of English can form a unified profession. If college teachers of English are really engaged in the same professional activities as the elementary school teacher and the secondary school teacher of English, then they have an obligation to help guarantee that a humanistic approach to the teaching and learning of English informs the English classroom at every level.

5. Will the conversations which have begun among teachers of English from the United States, Canada, and the United Kingdom continue to be as fruitful as they have proved in the first few years of dialogue? The impact of the Dartmouth Seminar of 1966 has been apparent and great. How much change in the teaching of English will take place in the typical American school as a result of the continued sharing of experience is a major question for the next decade.

No single volume can answer so many questions satisfactorily. This one tries only to review answers which have been put forth since 1958 and to speculate about the future of English teaching on the basis of my own experience in the classroom and in the conference hall.

I should like to thank John H. Fisher, James R. Squire, Wallace W. Douglas, and Carl A. Barth for discussing sections of this book with me. The opinions it contains are my own, but they have been tempered and refined by the good will, patience, and wisdom of my friends.

Michael F. Shugrue
Modern Language Association
New York University

English in a Decade
of Change

chapter one

The English Curriculum

The State of the English Curriculum
The development of a curriculum for the English classroom must,
by its very nature, be a continuous, open-ended process. No
curriculum, however carefully designed and tested by teams
of scholars and classroom teachers, can be used with equal effectiveness in every kind of school by every kind of teacher for
every kind of pupil. Coming to first grade from a disadvantaged
home, the urban youngster for whom English is a second language
will not respond to curriculum materials in the same way as the
child with a rich linguistic background who comes to school
from an economically advantaged suburban community. Both
youngsters, however, do share an instinctive curiosity about
language and a capacity to expand their already considerably
sophisticated linguistic patterns which the teacher of English
must quickly tap. Although the student enrolled in a vocational
course of study in a community college may not bring to college the same motivation to learn or the same cultural background as the freshman entering a major university, he can be
brought to respond to literature and to develop and enrich his
linguistic skills if his teacher has prepared a curriculum to fit his
interests and needs.

Knowing what he wants to accomplish in his classroom and
how to achieve his goals is the constant curriculum problem of
the English teacher at any level. If he sees himself as a cus-
todian of literary masterpieces and information about literature
or considers language study to be the mastery of a particular

formal grammar, he will quickly and deservedly lose the interest of his students. If, on the other hand, he has a broader vision of English teaching, he can help his students attain linguistic skill and literary sophistication. Once the English teacher has set goals for his students and selected the books and other media which he will use in class, he has begun to develop a curriculum. He refines his curriculum further as he decides how information and concepts will be introduced in the classroom. Will the teacher lecture regularly? Will students, through talk, discover principles for themselves? When the teacher faces new classes the next semester or fall, he revises his curriculum in the light of previous successes and failures and, most important, in the light of the students whom he now begins to teach.

Whenever textbooks are adopted for an entire municipal school system, state school system (as in California and twenty other states), or college course, the teacher must use his professional skills and his knowledge of his students to adapt the text for his own classes, to vary the suggested rate of progress, to change the emphases expressed by the authors, or even to abandon the text for newspapers, magazines, paperbacks, films, and television in order to reach and interest students. Although the textbook should never be more than one of many tools available to the teacher as he works to achieve educational goals, it often governs the activities of the English classroom if the teacher is poorly prepared, too busy to plan for himself, or simply not interested in his students. One cynical justification for system-wide and state-wide textbook adoptions, in fact, is the guarantee that any teacher who follows the book will be sure to cover at least a minimal amount of material in his classes. A more valid justification is the hope that a well-chosen textbook can provide the cornerstone for a sequential curriculum.

Even the well-prepared teacher, however, will find it difficult to set goals for his English program unless he continues to study professional literature about the English curriculum and the teaching of English in school and college. Although the task of keeping up with research and criticism has become increasingly difficult for the teacher over the last decade, he should occasionally turn to such an authoritative survey of curriculum trends as that written by James E. Miller, Jr. of the University of Chicago, former editor of *College English*, a member of the NCTE Commission on Literature, and the author of well-conceived and popular textbooks. Looking back over nearly 100 years of American educational history in 1967, Miller identified four stages in the development of an English curriculum: the authoritarian, progressive, academic, and humanitarian.[1]

He characterized the first of these by "the arid classicism and rote learning of the nineteenth century," a view of English familiar to any readers of this book who studied a prescriptive grammar based on Latin and literary masterpieces which were treated as artifacts to be admired for their workmanship but rarely enjoyed.

The inevitable reaction was progressive education, related, according to Miller, to "John Deweyism (something different from the real Dewey), indiscriminate permissiveness, and social adjustment, all running deep into the twentieth century." While this "life-adjustment" stage recognized that language was a medium of communication and a tool which every youngster should be able to use, it ignored the growth of the literary imagination and removed most of the content of English from the English classroom. To be able to speak well on the telephone or ask for a date proved no substitute for rich literary experiences and linguistic sophistication.

The third great influence on the curriculum, which Miller characterizes as "a revolution in our schools which we may, for convenience, date from Russia's Sputnik launching in 1957," led to the introduction of "the new math, the new physics, and the new English in our schools, together with emphasis on intellectual grouping or tracking to identify and challenge the intellectually gifted—all rather much under the supervision of the academic rather than the education establishment, and all somewhat a reaction to the academically thin curricula of the schools awash in the back eddies of extremist progressivism." Much of this chapter will be devoted to the development of the "content curriculum" now beginning to have a major influence on the teaching of English throughout the United States.

Even before a curriculum which emphasized the content of

English could reach large numbers of the nation's schools, however, a new notion of English had appeared. The humanitarian view, which places "literature, defined in the broadest terms, at the center of the curriculum" and takes "the development of the imagination, conceived in the most liberating sense, as its ultimate aim," emerged from the Anglo-American Conference on the Teaching and Learning of English held at Dartmouth College in the summer of 1966, a conference which emphasized creative English programs and expressed grave doubts about the value of content-oriented programs either for academically gifted or for culturally and economically deprived students. The impact of the Dartmouth Seminar reports on current curriculum planning in English will, of course, be a central concern of this chapter.

Because the third stage—the academic—has dominated the thinking and planning of the last ten years, it deserves a detailed description and evaluation. Quite clearly the content curriculum will influence American schools and colleges throughout the 1970's. We must ask how it will change current English programs, whether the changes will be desirable, and how the lessons of the Dartmouth Seminar can be incorporated into new programs.

Why Reform in English?

Reform in English began none too soon. Unknowing administrators, unprepared teachers, unconcerned college professors, and an unaware public had allowed a curriculum which had neither proper direction nor valid substance to dominate the school English program. Many administrators, faced with an alarming shortage of qualified English teachers as more students entered and stayed in school, accepted—even if they knew better—the notion that "anybody can teach English" and assigned English classes to the history teacher, the gym instructor, and the guidance counselor. With neither a knowledge of the subject of English nor of the special pedagogical skills required to teach it, these hapless, overworked teachers struggled through the school day by relying heavily on textbooks and workbooks. Even many "English teachers," as the NCTE studies which will be discussed in the next chapter showed, lacked enough background in their field to plan a satisfactory curriculum. In addition, college and university professors of English maintained their aloofness from the schools. Without direction from the universities, with a constant turnover of ill-prepared teachers, and with burgeoning enrollments, school department chairmen and principals placed their faith in the textbook. If textbooks in English had been outstanding, the plight of the English classroom would have been less precarious. Well-intentioned authors, however, had ignored the linguistic and critical discoveries of the scholarly community, scrupulously avoided the dangers of controversy and censorship, and produced, instead, textbooks for the school which were outmoded, timid, and intellectually unsatisfactory.

James J. Lynch and Bertrand Evans published their influential and devastating *High School English Text-Books: A Critical Examination* in 1963. That report, prepared under the sponsorship of the Council for Basic Education with support from the Old Dominion Foundation, pinpointed objections to the textbook which had been increasing since 1958.

Although Lynch and Evans supported a somewhat too rigidly academic view of English, they presented detailed evidence of the serious inadequacies in the principal literature anthologies and grammar and composition books used in American schools. They objected to the "excessive reliance upon a spate of non-literary, non-fictional, 'informational' materials more suitable at their best to the daily newspaper than to a hard-covered, sturdily constructed anthology with a presumed claim to longevity exceeding twenty-four hours" and condemned "the solicitous urge to make anthologies 'easier' and thus more palatable to 'reluctant' and other readers who otherwise might shy away from more substantial challenges to their intelligence, sensitivity, and endurance, and give up reading altogether."[2] They found anthologies "overorganized" and filled with "extensive introductions and other editorial machinery" which "overwhelm to the point of obliteration the puny examples to which they address themselves." The authors also criticized severely the insensitive abridgment of poems and plays typical of many of the books. No matter what his abilities or background, the student could only find the anthologies burdensome and boring.

The language and composition books common to the English classroom contributed even more to the deadly repetitiousness of English. Lynch and Evans noted that the most popular texts gave a topic *"essentially the same treatment in any volume of any particular series that is given in the other volumes of that series."* Progressive education had introduced polite speech, social behavior, and motivational material into so many English textbooks that the authors found it "painfully apparent that the subject of English has lost its way in a wilderness of things, has become intolerably amorphous, unteachable, and undeserving of anyone's respect as a legitimate and discrete school subject." Their criticisms reflected an anger and sense of frustration common to many in the profession.

At the college level, the freshman English program continued to depend upon the handbook which stressed school grammar, correct usage, and the principles of expository writing. The typical college handbook was often indistinguishable from that which the student had used in high school. In sections of freshman English reserved for remedial work, students labored with handbooks and workbooks which repeated the exercises and lessons of earlier years.

Although Marjorie Smiley at Hunter College and Daniel Fader at the University of Michigan, among others, have shown since 1963 that relevance is as important to the English classroom as "the very best ever thought and written in the spirit of the humanistic tradition and the Anglo-American heritage," Lynch and Evans did demonstrate incontrovertibly that the typical English textbook of the early 1960's was a totally unsatisfactory curriculum guide. The knowledgeable teacher of English—of whom there were too few in the schools—was forced to use the textbook in school or college only cautiously and selectively. The English profession, however, had already begun to redefine the nature of English studies and the content of the English curriculum.

Solving the "Basic Issues"

As early as 1955, George Winchester Stone, who became Executive Secretary of the Modern Language Association in 1956, J. N. Hook, then Executive Secretary of the National Council of

Teachers of English, and other distinguished scholars and teachers were troubled enough by the state of English instruction in the schools to initiate discussions on a national level. In January 1958, three months after Russia's Sputnik I had focused the attention of the American public upon the need for excellence in education in modern society, the first of four important conferences on the basic issues in the teaching of English took place in New York City. With support from the Ford Foundation, twenty-eight scholars and teachers came together because, as they later reported, "Some of us in the profession believe that a thorough re-examination of the whole problem of the teaching of English, from the elementary grades through the graduate school, is now imperative. We think that as an initial step we need a clear formulation of the *Basic Issues* which confront us. We have undertaken to prepare this formulation, and we present it herewith. . . . We are talking, moreover, about Basic Issues, not about problems which would arise in reaching a solution if we had agreed upon what the solution should be. Two kinds of issues emerge, those *within* the profession and those *between* the profession and other interested parties, including the general public. . . . Our only vested interest is the development of an increasingly higher degree of literacy in young American citizens. We think the matter is urgent; we hope that the profession will see these issues as basic and will expeditiously find solutions for the problems arising from them."[3] In the course of four conferences, those who participated in the discussions agreed upon thirty-five issues on the curriculum, the preparation of English teachers, the role of English in American society, and the need for support for basic research. The influence of the seventeen issues dealing with the preparation of teachers of English will be discussed later in this volume. Those dealing with the curriculum have mapped the course of English studies since 1958. Even before Jerome S. Bruner's influential *The Process of Education* (1960), the Basic Issues conferees affirmed their belief in "an education in English which is sequential and cumulative in nature, practically and socially useful, and permanently rewarding to the mind and spirit of those who are fortunate enough to get it."

The participants acknowledged that "the fundamental liberal discipline of English" had been replaced "at some levels of schooling, by *ad hoc* training in how to write a letter, how to give a radio speech, manners, dating, telephoning, vocational guidance." While the first issue—*What is English?*—is again being hotly debated as the result of the Dartmouth Seminar, the tentative conclusions reached in the *Basic Issues Report* have governed almost every attempt to define English in the 1960's. Although the general agreement that "English composition, language, and literature are within our province" obviously did not settle "whether our boundaries should include world literature in translation, public speaking, journalism, listening, remedial reading, and general academic orientation," it strengthened the concept of the tripod of language, literature, and composition in English and enabled teachers to plan a curriculum different from and better than that current in the schools. Most English teachers would agree readily that the field of English includes language, literature, and composition as well as the skills of listening, speaking, reading, and writing, but even experts would be hard pressed to explain how each of these areas is to be introduced into the classroom and related to all of the others. *Freedom and Discipline in English,* the 1965 report of the Commission on English, explained that "language, primarily the English language, constitutes the core of the subject" and that "the study and use of the English language is the proper content of the English curriculum."[4] More recently, Harold B. Allen has reemphasized the primacy of language in the study of English: English is *"the study of the English language and of its use as a medium of communication."* Professor Allen extends *use* to include "all instances from the most trivial utterances or simplest direction to the most majestic productions of our literature, both spoken and written, both as produced and as received."[5]

Still most widely accepted as a standard definition of English studies in the United States, however, is that presented as the twelfth recommendation of *Freedom and Discipline.* Heavily influenced by the *Basic Issues Report,* it urges "that the scope of the English program be defined as the study of language, literature, and composition, written and oral, and that matters not clearly related to such study be excluded from it." Yet that definition fails to emphasize the integrated nature of language, literature, and composition, written and oral. Moreover, its emphasis on English as a *study* neglects a central point made by those who attended Dartmouth—that English, however defined, is first of all an experience with language, written and oral. Neither the *Basic Issues Report* nor any other statement can hope to define English once and for all. Accepting the tripod, however, has made it possible for English teachers to develop an English curriculum with clearer goals and fewer peripheral activities.

Those who have been most active in the construction of the English curriculum since 1958 have answered a second basic question raised by the *Basic Issues Report* with a resounding "Yes." As late as 1963 Lynch and Evans were distressed by the repetitiveness of the language and composition books used in secondary schools and would have been equally distressed if they had studied those used in the colleges. The Basic Issues participants had asked to what extent the teacher at any level should be able to make assumptions about the training which his students had received at lower levels. Most of the curriculum research of the past decade has tried to answer the formal question, "*Can basic programs in English be devised that are sequential and cumulative from the kindergarten through the graduate school?*" The conferees recognized that this issue was crucial to the entire document and to any serious approach to change in the curriculum: "Unless we can find an answer to it, we must resign ourselves to an unhappy future in which the present curriculum disorder persists and the whole liberal discipline of English continues to disintegrate and lose its character." A sequential curriculum could only be possible if there were wide agreement on a body of knowledge and set of skills which would be standard at certain points in the curriculum. Furthermore, any sequence would have to allow for flexibility of planning, individual differences, and varying patterns of growth. The products of the Curriculum Study and Demonstration Centers in English funded by the Cooperative Research Branch of the United States Office of Education beginning in 1962 reflect the national effort to develop the sequence which the *Basic Issues Report* considered so fundamental.

The advocates of a sequential, articulated, cumulative, spiral curriculum in English found strong support in Jerome S. Bruner's enormously popular and influential *The Process of Education* (1960), a report which emerged from a conference of thirty-five scientists and educators who had gathered at Woods Hole on Cape Cod to consider ways to improve the teaching of science in the elementary and secondary schools.

Bruner noted "a renewed interest in complex learning of a kind that one finds in schools, learning designed to produce general understanding of the structure of a subject matter" and recognized that the "construction of curricula proceeds in a world where changing social, cultural, and political conditions continually alter the surroundings and the goals of schools and their students." [6] Advocating the cultivation of excellence as the most general objective of education, he warned that "it should be clear in what sense this phrase is used. It here refers not only to schooling the better students but also to helping each student achieve his optimum intellectual development. Good teaching that emphasizes the structure of a subject is probably even more valuable for the less able student than for the gifted one, for it is the former rather than the latter who is most easily thrown off the track by poor teaching." His emphasis on reaching every student has become as essential a consideration in curriculum planning in English as the search for an underlying structure in the field. Bruner defended teaching the student "initially not a skill but a general idea, which can then be used as a basis for recognizing subsequent problems as special cases of the idea originally mastered" rather than insisting on "the mastery of facts and techniques" as the best way to make the materials students are exposed to count in their thinking. Most important for English, he accused the schools of wasting precious years by postponing the teaching of many important subjects on the ground that they are too difficult and emphasized that "the foundations of any subject may be taught to anybody at any age in some form." The Physical Science Study Committee programs developed by Jerrold Zacharias and Educational Services,

Inc. bear out, at least for the sciences, Bruner's declaration that a continual deepening of one's understanding of basic ideas comes from learning to use them in progressively more complex forms.

Bruner emphatically asserted that literature as well as the sciences and social sciences could be taught with an emphasis upon the intuitive grasp of ideas and upon the use of basic ideas because "intellectual activity anywhere is the same, whether at the frontier of knowledge or in a third-grade classroom." He called for the best minds in every discipline to be put to work to design a curriculum in which the method of discovery of general principles would lead to progressively more difficult problems, in which what is learned in the early grades has relevance for later learning, and in which children become more actively alert to how things affect or are connected with each other. In his analysis of Jean Piaget's stages in the intellectual development of the child, Bruner pointed out that "the intellectual development of the child is no clockwork sequence of events; it also responds to influences from the environment, notably the school environment" and argued that instruction "need not follow slavishly the natural course of cognitive development in the child," but should "lead intellectual development by providing challenging but usable opportunities for the child to forge ahead in his own development." In his explanation of the spiral curriculum, for which his book is best known, Bruner specifically attacked the problem of teaching literature: "If it is granted, for example, that it is desirable to give children an awareness of the meaning of human tragedy and a sense of compassion for it, is it not possible at the earliest appropriate age to teach the literature of tragedy in a manner that illuminates but does not threaten? There are many possible ways to begin: through a retelling of the great myths, through the use of children's classics, through presentation of and commentary on selected films that have proved themselves. Precisely what kinds of materials should be used at what age with what effect is a subject for research— research of several kinds."

Because Bruner's description of the spiral curriculum was intellectually exciting, because he offered a framework for the kind of sequence called for by the *Basic Issues Report*, and because he addressed himself directly to the teaching of English in the schools, Bruner's theories have had an enormous impact on the curriculum work done by the Study and Demonstration Centers in English. Although G. Robert Carlsen and James Crow, in a preliminary review of the work of several Curriculum Study Centers, reported that the staff at Florida State University, "After seriously grappling with the Brunerian idea of the 'inner structure of the discipline' and the spiral curriculum" had concluded "that the idea is too foggy to be of much help in structuring a course of study," [7] Bruner touched upon matters which no one designing an English curriculum can afford to ignore. Of obvious importance are Bruner's convictions that what is taught be worth teaching, that repetition and the accumulation of facts do not constitute a satisfactory curriculum in any subject, that the discovery method—inductive teaching—must be fostered in the classroom, that the child's intuitive powers must be developed in his school experiences, and that media and technological advances must be used appropriately in the classroom to allow the teacher to accomplish more effectively his task as communicator, model, and identification figure through the use of a wide variety of devices which "expand experience, clarify it, and give it personal significance." When James Miller advocates that "the English curriculum from beginning to end should have as its primary aim the education, development, and fullest possible extension of the linguistic imagination" and should emphasize "the primacy of creativity and imagination in learning to live as a full participant in the vital world of language," he has complemented Bruner's call to develop the intuitive powers of the youngster through experience and discovery in the classroom.[8] Bruner's notions about an inner structure and a spiral have profoundly influenced those in English who have attempted to challenge students with ideas rather than facts and those who have tried to plan a curriculum which frees the student from the repetitive learning still typical of most English programs.

English teachers trying to discover an inner structure in English could also turn to the work of Northrop Frye. In such works as *The Anatomy of Criticism,* Frye speculated that the curriculum might be organized by the "pre-generic" forms he defines—Comedy, Romance, Tragedy, and Irony. Defending the notion of sequence in English at the annual meeting of the MLA in 1963, Frye observed, "I think it should be possible to work out a curriculum for [those stages of education between learning to read and college] which will treat literature as a progressive and systematic study, and which will furnish the student with something of tangible and permanent value at whatever stage he drops out of it." [9] He argued that "random patching of the existing curricula, though it may have a practical look, is no longer practical. The only thing that is practical now is to gain a new theoretical conception of literature." He then outlined the main principles of a coherently organized curriculum: "Poetry should be at the centre of all literary training, and literary prose forms the periphery. In a properly constructed curriculum there would be no place for 'effective communication' or for any form of utilitarian English." He urged that the "physical energy and concrete vividness of verse" normally be presented earlier than "the more complex and adulterated rhythms of prose." Frye also discussed the obligation of the teacher of writing to encourage an inductive process which fosters in the student "the feeling of self-expression, the power of developing a new skill, the growing sense of mastery in making all those strange new words say what one means" while keeping a deductive frame of reference behind it. Like Bruner, Frye contributed seminal ideas to the work of the Study Centers, especially to that at the University of Nebraska. The beliefs that a sequence could be found for English and that discovery should be the principal road into the subject strengthened the determination of those working to improve English in the schools. Frye's emphasis on teaching Comedy and Romance in the early years and Tragedy and Irony later even established a rude framework for a structured English curriculum.

At least seven of the Study and Demonstration Centers have tried to answer the question raised in the ninth basic issue: *"How should the basic program in English be modified for the less able student?"* At the heart of this question, we see today, is a recognition that the curriculum must be flexible enough to challenge students not only of varying intellectual abilities but of different cultural, social, economic, and linguistic backgrounds. Surprisingly enough, however, the *Basic Issues Report* did not consider the problems of educating the disadvantaged youngster, problems since discussed perceptively in *Improving English Skills of Culturally Different Youth in Large Cities* (1964) and in the NCTE's *Language Programs for the Disadvantaged* (1965). The Basic Issues conferees realized that the English program in the schools must reach every child, but did not foresee the national movement to free the ghetto from intellectual and cultural as well as economic blight. The disadvantaged or deprived child has become in this decade the primary target for educational experimentation. As recently as 1962, however, Marjorie Smiley of Hunter College could note that although the education of underprivileged children in great cities had been talked about since as early as 1809, research until that time had "very little" to say about teaching these children, "certainly much less than the dimensions and the seriousness of the problem demand."

"Since these children are in certain specific ways *deprived*," she wrote, "their total educational program and especially their programs in English must first of all provide special compensations. . . . Their school and teachers need to help extend the world of these children with more *varied experiences* than their circumscribed lives afford." Furthermore, they need *"much more practice* in the many phases of language readiness that teachers take for granted among middle-class children." [10]

In 1965 the NCTE Task Force on Teaching English to the Disadvantaged, a team of twenty-two scholars and teachers, observed and described in detail 190 programs for the disadvantaged, both rural and urban, throughout the United States. In four months members of the team visited 115 districts and agencies in sixty-four cities and towns to meet "the great need of the moment" for "information about the hundreds of independent and uncoordinated programs in language and reading for the disadvantaged that had sprung up in every part of the country." [11] The ten recommendations of the Task Force spelled out better than any previous document specific ways to improve the teaching of English to disadvantaged youngsters. The Task Force urged "that children be permitted to operate in the dialect of

their community at the lower levels of elementary school education, and that direct instruction in the use of standard informal
English be begun no earlier than the intermediate elementary
grades." It advised "that oral language receive greater stress in
language instruction for the disadvantaged at all levels of education, from preschool through adult" and that "at all levels of
instruction the English curriculum for disadvantaged students
include appropriate imaginative literature chosen and presented
with these students in mind." While it focused on a special segment of the school population, the Task Force joined with the
Basic Issues Report, with Bruner, and with Frye, to urge the
development of "adequate structure and continuity throughout
all levels of school, from preschool through twelfth grade," a
task it saw as the "responsibility of the school district."

Federal Support Comes to English

Although individual schools and school districts across the United
States are constantly engaged in systematic curriculum planning
and revision, no one school or system can influence national
curriculum trends and the kinds of textbooks which publishers
commission and publish for the schools. Indeed, one great strength
of the American educational system is the local autonomy which
gives a distinctive character to the one high school in York,
Nebraska, and to the four high schools in Lincoln, Nebraska,
only fifty miles away. Significant changes in the curriculum
ordinarily reach large numbers of school systems very slowly. In
the last six years, however, sweeping changes have been occurring
in some parts of the United States as a result of the English
Program of the Office of Education. As the federal government
began funding curriculum research projects in English early in
1962, some critics of federal support worried aloud about the
dangers of federal interference in school programs and about a
nationally imposed curriculum. As the products of the two dozen
Study and Demonstration Centers began to appear in 1966, however, it became abundantly clear even to the doubters that no
such federal interference was intended or had taken place. The
multiplicity of materials, the variety of interests and populations,
and the uniqueness of some approaches have provided the best

evidence that research into the nature of the English curriculum had been governed only by the imagination and capacity of hundreds of dedicated scholars and teachers. A survey of the achievements of Project English or the English Program of the USOE, as it came to be known later, provides an unparalleled view of the extensive and varied curriculum projects which have been underway for more than five years and suggests the principal directions of English studies in the schools—and in the colleges—for the next decade. A close look at the work of the Study Centers at the University of Nebraska, Northwestern University, Hunter College of the City of New York, the University of Oregon, and Carnegie-Mellon University, and the proceedings and publications of the Dartmouth Seminar will provide a balanced view of directions in English curriculum planning.

An address delivered by Ralph C. M. Flynt, then Associate Commissioner for Educational Research and Development in the USOE, to a conference of chairmen of college English departments in Washington, D.C. at the end of the first year of Project English and a first report on Project English by J. N. Hook in *PMLA* (September 1963) provide the historical background for the Office of Education's English Program, as well as expressing the hopes of the English profession for significant curriculum change, reinforcing the central concerns of the *Basic Issues Report*, and providing a yardstick for measuring the work of the past few years. Flynt discussed "the mutual efforts of the community of English scholars, teachers of English and the Office of Education in the enterprise we have come to call Project English . . . our first venture in the area of programmed curriculum research and development." [12] He promised that "with your support and with the growing involvement of the English scholar, Project English will long endure." Commissioner Flynt's enthusiasm and sincerity cannot be questioned despite the directions currently being taken by the Office of Education, directions which threaten the continuation of any substantive curriculum development in English. This changing official attitude, a phenomenon which became increasingly apparent throughout 1967, will be traced later in our discussion. At this point one can only note the hopeful, optimistic, and sincere observations of

Mr. Flynt: Project English was "an expression of the growing Federal concern for excellence in education," a concern which is part of the long encouragement in the United States both of scientific endeavor and of educational enterprise. By tying Project English to earlier efforts to support research and to improve educational facilities, Flynt committed the Office of Education to the improvement of English instruction at all levels. He noted that "Scholars and teachers had long realized that English teaching has been steadily hampered by insufficient research, too little experimentation, insufficient dissemination of what is known, and uncertainty about the best ways to deal with the tremendous complexities of the language, the multitudinous literary selections that might conceivably enrich learning, and the great differences among children themselves." He acknowledged, further, the influence of both the Basic Issues Conferences and the 1961 NCTE *National Interest and the Teaching of English* in stimulating the government to support "the development of a new, articulated curriculum for English" designed by English scholars and educators. He also attacked "the cluttered sequence of courses which today is sometimes called 'English' " and anticipated that "the new English curriculum will be devoted substantially to language, composition, and literature." He observed in summary, "We now find that elementary and secondary and college teachers of English are approaching agreement that their task is threefold and that they should concentrate on an integrated program of instruction in the nature and characteristics of the English language, the improvement of written and spoken composition, and the reading of the best materials that children at a given point of development are able to comprehend." Flynt's use of such key words as articulated, sequential, and integrated, his acceptance of the tripod of language, literature, and composition, and his call to eliminate the "cluttered sequence" demonstrated again the influence of the *Basic Issues Report* and the direction which English had begun to take toward a "beefed-up," content-oriented curriculum for the schools.

J. N. Hook, who had served as the first of four Coordinators of Project English (the others were Erwin Steinberg of Carnegie-

Mellon, John Gerber of the University of Iowa, and Lewis Leary of Columbia University), reviewed other attempts by the profession to awaken Congress to the need to provide support for research in English above the shoestring level. Hook reminded his audience that when the National Defense Education Act provided federal funds for the improvement of instruction in science, mathematics, and the foreign languages in 1958, the NCTE had testified before Congress about the great needs in the field of English. The call for federal support issued in the *Basic Issues Report* and the effective testimony of the NCTE led Congress in September 1961 to authorize limited expenditures for the improvement of English instruction through the use of funds administered by the Cooperative Research Branch of the Office of Education under Public Law 531. A conference called in February of 1962 outlined goals and directions for the new Project English and enabled the Office of Education to fund six Curriculum Study Centers by April of that year: Carnegie-Mellon University (then Carnegie Institute of Technology), Hunter College of the City of New York, the University of Minnesota, Northwestern University, the University of Nebraska, and the University of Oregon. In its first year, Project English also sponsored conferences on professional problems, including the important meeting in May 1962 in Pittsburgh on "Needed Research in the Teaching of English," funded more than thirty basic and applied research projects in English, and made plans for Demonstration Centers (with four funded in 1963 at the University of California at Berkeley, New York University, Syracuse University, and Western Reserve University in cooperation with Euclid Central Junior High School). In 1963 additional Curriculum Study Centers were established at Florida State University, the University of Georgia, Teachers College of Columbia University, and the University of Wisconsin. Surveying the first months of activity, Professor Hook noted four principal needs in English:

> 1) Through curriculum study centers and research projects we need to answer as many as possible of the big unanswered questions concerning the teaching of English, . . . [including] how to develop curriculum patterns that will take into account both the logical sequence of our subject and the varying rates

at which children develop. 2) We need to find ways of increasing the knowledge and the competence of teachers now in the classroom [through such effective instruments as institutes, seminars, in-service programs, and improved supervision.] 3) We need to improve present programs for preparing teachers of English. 4) We need a better system of disseminating information about what we already know concerning the teaching and learning of English, and about many of the good things now going on in the classrooms of the nation.[13]

These goals are still pertinent—even crucial—ones for the profession. The exhilaration of the profession late in 1963 can scarcely be overestimated. The federal government had finally recognized its obligations to the humanities and had, with significant amounts of money, begun a program to improve instruction in English through basic research. At that point in time no one could foresee that the war in Vietnam would severely limit funds for educational research and that the early achievements of Project English might be not the beginning of a national commitment to quality in English instruction but, sadly enough, an isolated high-water mark in the history of the relationship between the federal government and the scholarly community.

The original Curriculum Study Centers have completed the research they undertook early in 1962. Carnegie-Mellon, under the direction of Erwin Steinberg and Robert Slack, developed a curriculum in language, literature, and composition for the able college-bound student in grades ten to twelve in its first years and then modified that curriculum to make it suitable for average as well as able students. Marjorie Smiley at Hunter College focused on an English program for the culturally disadvantaged in the junior high school years. Stanley Kegler at Minnesota prepared thirty-one resource units in language for the junior and senior high school while Wallace Douglas investigated the teaching of composition from seventh grade through the first two years of college. Albert Kitzhaber at the University of Oregon used the Portland Study as a base for a well-balanced, sequential program in language, literature, and composition for the senior high school, and Paul Olson and Frank

Rice at Nebraska, ambitious as only midwesterners can be, began to develop a total curriculum for grades K-13, emphasizing composition and rhetoric, but weaving in strands of literature and language. In each Study Center, college professors of English were deeply committed to the design of an effective English program for the schools.

Erwin R. Steinberg, who became the second Coordinator of Project English, prepared the official record of the May 1962 conference at Carnegie-Mellon University on "Needed Research in the Teaching of English." Although most professors of English who attended the conference felt "decidedly out of their element" in undertaking curriculum development, Dean Steinberg noted that the conferees were able to identify difficult research problems which needed the attention of the scholarly community.[14] Their desire to find appropriate methods and techniques for the effective teaching of language in the English classroom led directly to curriculum materials developed by the Centers at Oregon, Minnesota, and Nebraska, to name only three. Influenced by the *Basic Issues Report* and by Bruner's concepts of inner structure and of the spiral curriculum, the participants sought to identify "the structure and sequence inherent on the one hand in various subject matters and skills and on the other in the maturing intelligence and abilities of the student—and their interrelationships. . . ." The curriculum materials later written at Oregon and at Nebraska are two excellent examples of the sequential, articulated, cumulative, spiral curriculum which the conferees discussed in 1963.

Late in 1963 Dean Steinberg could report on a thriving Project English. With the addition of Indiana University and the University of Illinois the number of Study Centers had risen to twelve. Funds had been approved to support the preparation of authoritative texts of the published work of Mark Twain under John Gerber at the University of Iowa. Steinberg could assure the profession that proposals for research in English were being reviewed by specialists in English who served the Office of Education as advisers to the Commissioner of Education. In addition to surveying what had already been initiated, Steinberg recommended that more attention in future years be paid "to curriculum development in English at the elementary school level" and urged, further, that there "be at least one center concerned with the basic English course required of all undergraduates and another concerned with the curriculum for the undergraduate major in English." He called for studies of the curriculum for the Ph.D. in English, the Ph.D. in English Education, and the Ed.D. in English Education and asked his peers in college English departments to participate in the design of programs for the culturally disadvantaged: "Some of the ablest people in our profession ought to see this as our responsibility and not one to be left to the social scientists. The central problems here are language, literacy, and the traditions of our society, and how to make them meaningful and useful to people for whom even now they have little meaning or use." He observed that there "is no group better equipped to address itself to this problem than members of college and university departments of English working with their counterparts in the public schools."

Dean Steinberg could single out the Allerton Park Conference on Research in the Teaching of English, sponsored by the University of Illinois in December 1962, as one of the major achievements of Project English. As Robert W. Rogers noted in his opening remarks to the eighty chairmen and other representatives of college and university departments of English who gathered in the library of the Allerton mansion near Monticello, Illinois, "Collectively we represent large resources of learning, prestige, and wealth. . . . What we do here, or fail to do, will be widely noticed. . . . If we declare that the most prestigious members of English departments should work in programs specifically designed for teachers, we must be prepared to 'encourage' our own luminaries to do so. If we declare for a Ph.D. in the teaching of English, we must return to our own campuses and get the slow-moving curricula machinery going. If we assert that notable contributions to the work of training teachers make for valid claims to promotion, we must practice this precept in our own departments." [15] John H. Fisher provided an even wider context for the Allerton discussions: "I submit that until we in college departments can come to grips sincerely and realistically with the uses of literature and the relationship between literary study and the teaching of literacy, we can take no meaningful part in a national program for the improvement of English" (p.21). Among the eleven resolutions adopted by the seminar participants was a call for the chairmen of college and university English departments to organize a "permanent national association" of chairmen of departments in American colleges and universities. Through the Association of Departments of English or ADE, as it is now known, more than half of the departments in the United States have been able to establish a continuing dialogue on the problems of administration, the supply of and demand for faculty, and the undergraduate and graduate curriculums. The Allerton Conference demonstrated the most effective kind of federal support—from a federally-sponsored seminar emerged a self-supporting, responsible professional association.

If the departmental chairman's role was once the left-handed activity of the distinguished scholar taking his turn as an administrator, it had clearly become a profession in itself in the years of expanding enrollments which followed the Second World War. As Professor Rogers observed in an address to fifty-five new chairmen attending an ADE Seminar at Pennsylvania State University in 1967, "Ideally, in academic life, the departments should have a collective responsibility for leadership, with the chairman acting only as an executive agent who carries out the will of his colleagues. . . . Unhappily the complexities of administration in higher education make this traditional pattern of academic governance largely impossible; the day of the amateur has passed. A chairman now must be cognizant of the main developments in the discipline and profession of English in order to insure the relevance of his department's work and to select for his faculty the most promising, vital, lively teachers and scholars that the profession can offer." [16] By the early 1960's it was possible for a chairman to have a faculty of more than 100 professors, a graduate student enrollment approaching 500, and more than 5,000 students taking just the freshman English courses in his department. In addition, the competent chairman found himself writing proposals for summer institutes for the retraining of school teachers, establishing articulation programs with elementary and secondary schools and with the junior and community colleges in his area, and serving on committees and commissions for the Office of Education and for his professional associations. Today's chairman is not only asked to be a scholar-teacher, but a man well versed in curriculum research, in the opportunities for federal assistance for graduate fellowships, research programs, and institutes, and in the myriad problems of administration. That the Allerton Park Conference generated an association of chairmen was important not only to the experienced chairmen facing new challenges but to the many new chairmen who take over departments of English each year. In the fall of 1967, for example, 241 new chairmen assumed office in senior colleges and universities and 143 new chairmen were appointed to office in the junior and community colleges.

1963 was indeed a year of achievement for the English profession. The first studies financed by the Office of Education under the Cooperative Research Program appeared and were widely read and well received. Ruth Strickland and Walter Loban's *The Language of Elementary School Children* demonstrated that research support for English could produce substantive studies of immense value to the profession. Richard Braddock, Richard Lloyd-Jones, and Lowell Schorer's *Research in Written Composition* not only surveyed hundreds of studies and identified the best of them, but directed the profession to major, unresolved problems in the teaching of writing.

As the number of Study and Demonstration Centers grew, it became apparent that they needed to exchange information and ideas and to inform the profession about the work they were undertaking. Accordingly, in May 1964, representatives from the Centers, from the MLA and NCTE, and from the Office of Education met at Carnegie-Mellon for the first of a series of yearly conferences which discussed the problems of copyrighting units prepared by the Centers, the commercial and noncommercial dissemination of experimental materials, and the testing of curriculum units in the schools. Although their programs were still in the experimental stage, the Study Center Directors agreed to allow the MLA and NCTE to distribute sample units to teachers attending NDEA summer institutes in 1965, 1966, and 1967. A licensing agreement with the Office of Education made possible the establishment of the English Institute Materials Center and the distribution of 111 sample units from eighteen Centers to nearly 15,000 elementary and secondary school teachers in 414 institutes. In addition, the EIMC supplied staff members and participants in institutes with yearly progress reports on the work of the Centers and a review of new research and training programs in English established by the Office of Education. The argument for providing information and a limited distribution of the curriculum units was clear: if new curriculums, founded largely on the principles of sequence and inner structure and incorporating the best of linguistic and literary studies, were under construction, teachers needed to be informed and involved as quickly as possible. An evaluation of the use of new materials in the institutes made in the summer of 1966 showed, however, that the experimental units had not been widely or well used. The evaluators recommended that the directors of summer institutes be given a systematic introduction to the nature, value, and use of EIMC materials and guidance in the selection of appropriate curriculum units. The Office of Education responded by funding a special institute in January 1967 which brought the directors of Study and Demonstration Centers together with the directors of NDEA institutes in Reading and English for 1967.[17] This imaginative use of federal funds to inform institute directors about new directions in the teaching of English illustrated the genuine commitment of the Office of Education to the improvement of English instruction which marked the first five years of Project English.

The *PMLA* report to the profession in September 1966 outlined the substantive and varied achievements of twenty-five Study and Demonstration Centers. The University of California at Los Angeles and the California State Department of Education were cooperating, for example, to produce teachers' guides for teaching English as a second language to pupils of elementary school age. Outlining a sequential series of lessons based on sound principles of modern linguistics, the guides have already proved an effective tool for teachers working with the many California children who speak Spanish as their native language. Other Centers were working on projects as different as the preparation of teachers, linguistics for the deaf, composition units based on generative grammar and psycholinguistic theory for grades seven through nine, and literature for disadvantaged adolescents. The work which the Cooperative Research Program was sponsoring could clearly affect every grade level and every kind of student before the decade was over. As each Center revised and tested its materials, it was able to formulate an increasingly thoughtful rationale for its curriculum. Most of the curriculums, however, were still not available to the classroom teacher or curriculum supervisor. In the fall of 1967 the MLA and NCTE had received permission from four Centers to make ten representative units available to the profession, but many—indeed most—of the interesting and novel curriculum materials remained inaccessible to the profession. The real impact of the Centers on the elementary and secondary schools of the United States could only come as their commercial publication began after 1967.

Disturbingly, some teachers had dismissed the work of the Centers as too content-oriented or not sufficiently novel before they had seen more than a small fraction of the rich variety of units being produced in more than twenty Centers. The fifty British and American scholars and teachers who participated in the Dartmouth Seminar, for example, had access only to those units which the EIMC had been able to distribute to NDEA institutes in the summer of 1967. As a result, many attacked the work of Project English as traditional and pedestrian without having studied the distinctive literature units produced by Gateway English or the inventive composition lessons written by the staff of the Center at Northwestern University. Some professional journals also published premature reviews of the Center curriculums. In the October 1967 issue of the *English Journal,* Professors Carlsen and Crow frankly admitted that they had been unable to obtain and examine more than "a portion of the total output of the Centers" [18] when they began their review in 1966. Their objection that there is "nothing startlingly new in the work of the Centers" suggests that the units on the generative rhetoric of the sentence developed by Francis Christensen for the Center at the University of Nebraska and the bilingual readiness units prepared at Hunter College had not been available to them. The observation that the materials of the Centers lack "concern for the learner and how he learns" reflects a lack of familiarity with the Gateway English materials and with the Northwestern composition units, to name only two. Their criticism of the Centers for their "lack of definite plans for evaluation of the materials being produced" indicates that volume four of the Carnegie-Mellon materials, *Evaluation*, and the 1964 Cooperative Research Report entitled *Curriculum Development and Evaluation in English and Social Studies* were not yet readily at hand. Professor Carlsen's reputation as teacher and writer could have led many classroom teachers to dismiss new curriculum materials from the Centers even before they had been published, to remain too easily contented with current curriculum materials, and to ignore the directions for improving the English program in the schools which the Centers indicated. Fortunately, other reviews and reports, based on more complete information, have now begun to appear. The work of each Center deserves thoughtful consideration by reviewers in professional journals and the attention of every classroom teacher of English.

In addition to approving federal support for research and for institutes in 1965, the Congress established a National Foundation on the Arts and Humanities by passing Public Law 89-209 in mid-September. Signed by the President on September 22, the act established two separate national endowments, one for the Humanities and one for the Arts, each with a Chairman and a National Advisory Council. The Act also established a Federal Council on the Arts and Humanities to coordinate the activities of the two endowments. Under the direction of William Gibson of New York University, the Center for Editions of American Authors became the recipient of the first grant made by the Endowment for the Humanities. The Center quickly commissioned critical editions of major literary works by Stephen Crane, Ralph Waldo Emerson, Nathaniel Hawthorne, William Dean Howells, Washington Irving, Henry David Thoreau, Mark Twain, and Walt Whitman. By 1968 the editions had begun to appear at the rate of approximately thirty volumes a year, making available authoritative texts for the schools as well as for the scholar. With continued Endowment support, more than 230 volumes will be in print by 1974.

1967 marked the end of the initial phase of support for basic research on the English curriculum. Fourteen of the Study Centers and five Demonstration Centers had completed their work and submitted final reports to the Office of Education. Such important individual research projects as James R. Squire's *Study of English Programs in Selected High Schools Which Consistently Educate Outstanding Students in English* and its successor, *A Study of English Programs in Selected British Secondary Schools*, had been completed and recommendations published on ways to improve the staffing, administration, and curriculum of secondary school English programs. Thomas Wilcox's *National Survey of Undergraduate English Programs* had already begun to contribute valuable information to the profession about current college English courses. Materials from the Center at the University of Minnesota had been demonstrated and evaluated by the Upper Midwest Regional Educational Laboratory in three Minnesota high schools. At this point, two thoughtful scholars reviewed the progress of the five years from 1962 to 1967 and tried to evaluate what had taken place.

In *College Composition and Communication* (October 1967), Albert Kitzhaber of the University of Oregon took "A Retrospective View" of "The Government and English Teaching." Kitzhaber listed seven distinct achievements of the Curriculum Study Centers: a sharper definition of English as a school subject, a philosophical integrity for the English curriculum, defensible structures and sequence for English, the incorporation of current scholarship in learning theory and in the substantive fields of English, the close involvement of experienced school teachers in the writing of new curriculums, better communication between school and college teachers of English, and profound effects upon the making of English textbooks. Kitzhaber stated firmly his conviction that "Project English, and especially that part of it concerned with the Curriculum Study Centers, has been a considerable success."[19]

Robert Shafer of Arizona State University chose to give a thoughtful, extended review to the work of an individual Study Center, that at Carnegie-Mellon University. Reviewing the materials produced by "the first of the Curriculum Study Centers

. . . to complete its work," he was able to devote almost as many pages to his discussion of the rationale and lessons of the Carnegie curriculum as other reviewers, handicapped by the inaccessibility of many units, could give to the work of a dozen Centers.[20] Shafer had the entire curriculum in hand as he analyzed in detail the rationale for the Carnegie program, its goals, and the specific aims of each year's work. While acknowledging that the curriculum "may be one of the most carefully planned programs to integrate the study of language, literature, and writing that has ever been proposed," Shafer chose to reserve judgment on whether the program was truly sequential and cumulative "until more precise operational definitions of these terms have been formulated." He noted that Carnegie subscribed to inductive teaching and learning but found that the Center failed to develop and test "literary, linguistic, and composing models, which will lead students to inquiry and ultimately to growth in the processes of thought." Shafer's judicious review of the Carnegie curriculum provided a model for future evaluations of the thousands of pages of curriculum materials which had been produced by the Study Centers.

Although the Office of Education has encouraged institutions to continue to submit proposals for further basic research into the elusive nature of the English curriculum, the Office no longer appears to be deeply committed to support for English or for any of the other disciplines. There are disturbing indications that the English Program of the Office of Education, despite its obvious successes, has run its course.

The Tri-University Project, which is bringing a small number of college professors of English and elementary school teachers into a close working relationship at the University of Nebraska, and the Triple-T Conferences on the training of teachers of teachers in all areas do indicate that the Office of Education is still vitally committed to the improvement of public education. In 1967, however, the Office showed less enthusiasm for discipline-oriented research programs than it had in a decade; moreover, it has relied more and more heavily upon professional education personnel instead of subject-matter specialists for staff and for the review of proposals. Continued research into such disciplines as English is essential, whether carried out through the Regional Educational Laboratories and the Research and Development Centers or through direct funding from the Cooperative Research Program. While the Education Professions Development Act of 1967 promises to provide funds for the improvement of teachers in all areas at all levels beginning in 1969, it must not be allowed to be used as a means of phasing out support for subject-matter institutes for teachers under the guise of introducing "bold" or "innovative" programs. The 105 English Institutes of 1965 and the 126 of 1966 had dwindled to 96 in 1967 and to 85 in 1968. The English profession cannot and should not become a lobbying force for a "share of the education pie." Yet the profession has a responsibility, particularly strong in college and university departments of English, to convince the Office of Education, the Congress, and the public that it is acting in the best and broadest public interest when it calls for federal support for research in English. The profession must explain the central role of English in American education to the Office of Education and to the National Endowments, continue to submit thoughtful proposals for research on the curriculum at all levels, stay informed about legislation which affects research opportunities in English, and be willing to work with and for the Office of Education to strengthen the place of English in society. The real gains of the Curriculum Study and Demonstration Centers and of individual research projects can be duplicated in the 1970's if the profession is alert and interested.

The questions which were raised by the participants at the Dartmouth Seminar about the value of the curriculum materials produced by the Centers and about the basic educational philosophies behind the work of the Centers indicate the need for prudent assessment of what has been accomplished during the first phase of Project English and for careful planning for a second phase. The English curriculum should always be in a state of flux generated by healthy scholarly questioning, continued research, and experience in the classroom. In *The Uses of English*, Herbert J. Muller observed that both the American and British educators attending the Dartmouth Seminar realized that there was "a great deal of deadwood in the English curriculum today" and acknowledged that the "Curriculum Study Centers have therefore been busy designing programs with sequences, extending from the last years of grade school through high school, which will assure a sounder, more comprehensive training." [21] But he reported that the "British showed little interest in these programs except worry over the very idea of a program—it smacked of the fixed syllabus they want to get rid of. They found it hard to realize that American college teachers can never take for granted even the limited acquaintance with the literary classics that they did." While warning that "Designers of new curriculums in English cannot bank on the hope of 'teacher-proof' materials that inspires some enthusiasts in the new mathematics and new science," Muller left open the possibility that a sequence for English could be devised. Those at Dartmouth would not, I think, have found the materials from Gateway English or from Northwestern University inimical to their concepts of English. The Dartmouth approach, however, could significantly modify some of the Center programs, those, for example, which emphasize linguistics as a classroom subject to be studied for its own sake rather than language as an activity within the classroom.

If the primary goal of scholars in the first phase of the English Program of the Office of Education was to assist in developing curriculums for the schools, their primary goal in a second phase might well be the reform of the college English curriculum. Thomas Wilcox's *National Survey of Undergraduate English Programs* has already begun to supply authoritative data on current course offerings and curriculum requirements in college English departments. Although the Wilcox report and its recommendations for improving the teaching of English at the college level will not be published until 1969, Professor Wilcox had by late in 1967 accumulated and begun to interpret the first reliable statistics on the administration, staffing, and curriculum of the college English department. His figures support many of the observations presented in 1965 in the NCTE volume on *The College Teaching of English,* but suggest that some others were far too optimistic. If, as Wilcox indicates, more than half of the departments preparing school teachers have no regular articulation

with the schools, then Wayne Booth had misjudged the situation
when he wrote that "the overwhelming majority of English
departments are now thoroughly committed to assuming a responsible role in the improvement of instruction at all levels.
. . . It can be said, then, that there is no longer any question
about whether the departmental offerings will be cluttered up,
as one recalcitrant chairman put it, with courses in teacher
training. The question is whether the inevitable involvement of
English departments in teacher training will be effective." [22]
Wilcox has discovered, moreover, that over forty percent of the
colleges offering teacher preparation still do not require linguistics or advanced composition of their prospective teachers.

While some institutions are eliminating the freshman composition program, Wilcox finds most institutions (93%) still require
some introductory sequence in language, literature, and composition. When these first offerings are carefully planned,
they are, as Hoyt Trowbridge says, "The most important parts of
the curriculum offered by any department of English. . . . These
courses are the base of the pyramid, the foundation on which
the whole structure rests. Even more important, they are the
courses in which teachers of English have their best chance—
with some students their only chance—to open the world of the
humanities to minds often ignorant of its value." [23]

When Wilcox reports that staffing is the major problem in
departments throughout the United States, he only confirms the
statistics reported by Don Cameron Allen in his report on the
Ph.D. in English and American Literature and evident from
even a casual perusal of the *Vacancy Lists* published by the
Association of Departments of English three times a year. The
Lists showed in 1967, for example, that more than 500 institutions were searching for more than 1,000 professors and were
competing almost frantically for specialists in linguistics and
Old and Middle English. Perhaps in part because the demand
for linguists far exceeds the supply, Wilcox discovered that many
colleges have done less with linguistics than good high schools.
Robert M. Gorrell is certainly correct in reporting that "Possibly the most important development of the past twenty
years—certainly the one which has attracted most public attention

—is the English teacher's long-delayed recognition of facts about language which students of linguistics and philology have known for perhaps a century," [24] but the Wilcox study suggests that the influence of modern linguistics has not been felt nearly as deeply by some departments as by others.

Like all good research, Wilcox's study asks as many questions as it answers. His report and recommendations will stimulate needed research in the teaching of English at the college level. The availability of staff, the mobility of the profession, the place of the female professor, directions in the curriculum, cooperation with the schools and with departments of education in the preparation of teachers, and teaching loads and working conditions will all need to be studied in the light of his authoritative data. A preliminary analysis of his data suggests immediately the need to study more closely such undergraduate offerings as the freshman course, the introductory literature sequence, the major, and the teaching major. With five years of practical experience in the design of new courses for the schools, dozens of professors of English now have the opportunity and the experience to experiment at the college and university level.

An outstanding example of thoughtful preparation for such a second phase has taken place at Carnegie-Mellon University under the direction of Erwin Steinberg and Robert Slack in cooperation with Allegheny Community College. The Study Center at Carnegie had demonstrated that college professors could work with teachers in the schools to improve the school curriculum for the secondary student. The Center Staff had developed a sequential, integrated curriculum in language, literature, and composition which could be learned by the average as well as by the able, college-bound student. Carnegie, recognizing that the English curriculum in the burgeoning junior and community colleges of Pennsylvania needed the same kind of careful attention, outlined a program in 1967 to design an English curriculum for the first two years of college which would build upon the materials already written for the secondary school and would involve the same kinds of close cooperation with junior college teachers which the Carnegie staff had developed with teachers in the Pittsburgh schools. While the Office of Education considers whether or not to fund this exciting program, Carnegie has begun, with the assistance of the Center for Education established by the Carnegie Corporation of New York in 1966, this novel curriculum experiment. The Center for Education has also provided the stimulus at Carnegie for a Doctor of Arts degree in English as well as in other fields which will help graduate students who are preparing to teach English at the college level or those who are preparing to become language arts supervisors or heads of departments in major high schools. The program, which will require two academic years beyond the bachelor's degree, will include a selective examination demonstrating the candidate's scholarly knowledge in English, an internship in an English project as special researcher, part-time instructor, or contributing curriculum designer, and a dissertation that grows out of applied research. Carnegie has successfully tied together its teacher preparation programs and its curriculum development projects.

A third innovative step at Carnegie involves the construction of a core program in the humanities, including English, for the new College of Humanities and Social Sciences. Many of the same professors who have worked on curriculum materials in English and in the social studies and are closely identified with the Doctor of Arts program are participating in the design of this core curriculum; these same professors in the humanities and social sciences are also launching a fourth project, a broadly-conceived Urban Affairs Program. The drive for excellence which Phase One of Project English brought to light at Carnegie has now been successfully extended to the improvement of the college curriculum. Carnegie-Mellon can serve as a model for hundreds of institutions which should commit themselves as totally to curriculum revision at the college level.

Before examining some of the curriculum "Overviews" which have been prepared by the Centers and trying to evaluate the work of the Centers in light of the discussions at Dartmouth, the growing accessibility of materials from the Centers, and the common directions recognizable in the publications of the major Centers, it will be instructive to trace the development of one Center and to measure its influence on its university, its state, and the nation. Although the Centers at Carnegie-Mellon or the University of Oregon easily lend themselves to such an examination, let us, rather, outline the growth of the most ambitious of all the Centers, that at the University of Nebraska, one of the first Centers funded in the spring of 1962 and the only one developing a sequential, articulated, cumulative, spiral curriculum from kindergarten through the first year of college. The story of Nebraska's bold enterprise is worth relating.

The Nebraska Experience

The desire to have teachers of English at all levels and from all parts of the state talking with one another regularly about the English curriculum led the Nebraska Council of Teachers of English to organize a Curriculum Study Committee in the spring of 1961. Members of the department of English at the University of Nebraska took leading roles in the work of the Committee from the beginning. Because the University was clearly the most important force for educational change in the sparsely-populated state and because the department of English had long maintained a tradition of excellence through the presence of such scholars and writers as Louise Pound, Thomas M. Raysor, Karl Shapiro, and James E. Miller, Jr., the involvement of professors of English in the Study Committee guaranteed its future success. Under the chairmanship of Paul Olson, at that time a junior member of the department of English, the Committee obtained a grant of $10,000.00 from the Woods Charitable Fund, a long-time friend to education in Nebraska and in Illinois, to conduct a two-week workshop at the University in August. Twenty teachers from all parts of Nebraska used that time to develop and draft *A Curriculum for English*, a 400-page guide to curriculum planning printed by the University of Nebraska Press in October 1961. Frank M. Rice, then Head of the English Department at Omaha Central High School and later Co-Director of the Nebraska Study Center, remembers that summer as "one of the busiest and most exciting times in my thirty years of teaching here in the State of Nebraska." The *Curriculum*, which aroused national interest, was only a blueprint for curriculum change in Nebraska, but it was impressive enough to convince the Woods Fund late in 1961 to grant $27,000.00 for an expanded summer institute at the University in 1962. The University administration willingly agreed to contribute staff time and to waive tuition for the forty-four teachers who would participate. All of these steps were taken before federal support for institutes in English was available.

During the fall of 1961, while getting the *Curriculum* ready for the University Press and negotiating with the Woods Fund, Professor Olson and a team from the Study Committee developed a prospectus for a five-year Nebraska Curriculum Study Center to present to the Office of Education in January 1962. In April, the University of Nebraska was designated as the first of the Cooperative Research Program Curriculum Development Centers in English and awarded approximately $250,000.00 over five years to allow the University to plan a sequential curriculum, to test it in pilot schools around Nebraska, to revise units, and to evaluate the project. The Nebraska proposal was not only the first one approved by the Office of Education but the only one accepted unanimously by readers evaluating proposals. The seed money contributed by the Woods Foundation undoubtedly contributed to the carefully developed proposal and certainly made possible the large-scale curriculum change which was to occur in Nebraska over the next five years. Although the College of Education at the University of Nebraska cooperated fully in plans for the Study Center, the University's department of English and Nebraska classroom teachers of English brought the Study Center to the state.

Forty-four experienced teachers gathered in Andrews Hall on the University campus in early June to begin an eight-week program of vigorous graduate work in English and curriculum development. A typical daily schedule included three morning classes: one emphasized the theory of an articulated curriculum and developed classroom techniques for teaching English; a second studied seminal literary works and the philosophy of literature; a third introduced teachers to a descriptive, structural approach to the study of the language. For at least one hour every afternoon the group viewed and discussed audio-visual materials which might be included in the curriculum. For the remainder of the afternoons, sub-committees discussed problems connected with the preparation of specific curriculum units: what works of literature should be taught in the third grade; how early should students begin to write; at what level should Shakespeare first be introduced. Evenings found the participants doing the extensive reading connected with their courses and writing or evaluating curriculum units. No other group of teachers at Nebraska that summer or in any of the summer institutes run by the Commission on English in 1962 worked harder or with more dedication than the team of teachers entrusted with developing the Nebraska curriculum.

When the tired participants left Lincoln in August, a core staff, led by Paul Olson and Frank Rice, remained to edit the units which had been written during the summer and to prepare them for experimental use in Nebraska schools. Rice, who had joined the faculty of the department of English at the University in June 1962 as a Co-Director of the Study Center, and Olson supervised the process of editing some 5,000 pages of material, including forty units for the elementary school and forty-two for secondary classrooms designed both for the teacher and for the pupil. They also commissioned such specialists in rhetoric as Francis Christensen of the University of Southern California to prepare lessons on the generative rhetoric of the sentence which could be tested by Nebraska teachers and revised in the light of classroom experience. The primary job of the Directors themselves was to put the pieces together, to form the individual units into a coherent, sequential curriculum. The units on the description of language, logic, formal rhetoric, and literary forms which were ready to be tested in classrooms in five different kinds of school systems in the fall of 1962 were organized into a curriculum which endeavored through its inductive approach to provide students with a sense of how to gather literary or linguistic evidence and how to formulate conclusions on the basis of such evidence.

The Nebraska Center proposed from the beginning to do work in seven areas related to composition: (1) composition and the usable portions of classical rhetoric; (2) composition and the possibility of a new rhetoric: the rhetorical possibilities of "discourse analysis" and recent British studies of the philosophical "grammar and logic" of language; (3) composition and its relation to structural and transformational grammar; (4) composition and close reading: the teaching of literature and its use as a rhetorical or structural model; (5) the construction of criteria and tests for the measurement of excellence in composition; (6) the analysis of levels of student maturity at which basic composition "habits" or "patterns of decision" are formed; and (7) the construction of criteria and tests for the correction of themes in the areas of syntax, logic, and persuasive strategy. Two typical units developed by teachers preparing units in 1962 and again in a Woods-supported institute in the summer of 1963 will indicate Nebraska's approach.

The ninth grade student who has been reading the *Odyssey* is asked to compare selected passages from several translations and to write an essay pointing out variations in writing style. Analysis of such matters as metaphor, clarity, diction, rhythm, and sentence construction not only calls for close reading of the texts and knowledge of poetic techniques, but gives the student an opportunity to display his command of a critical vocabulary and his ability to organize his argument. Two objections might be offered: the *Odyssey* is too difficult a work for all but the most able students at the ninth grade level; the assignment is too highly structured and stresses expository writing at the expense of creative response.

In the tenth grade unit on "Man's Picture of Nature," the student, after studying the history of the creation as it is given in the *Book of Genesis* in the Old Testament, is asked to compare it with other accounts of the creation found in Indian legends, Greek and Roman mythology, and Norse mythology. Ideally, the student will not only learn to handle the techniques of comparison and contrast in expository prose, but to think more critically about the nature of man's existence in the world. Although the lesson allows the class to explore works outside of British and American literature, it places a considerable burden on the teacher who must choose good translations of the myths and legends which are to be presented to students.

Five school systems agreed to provide classrooms in which the

Nebraska materials could be tested for difficulty and for their appropriateness for students of varying maturity and cultural and economic backgrounds: a wealthy suburban system, Omaha Westside; an urban school system, Omaha itself; a large, middle-class city system, Lincoln; an experimental university system, University High School and Bancroft Elementary School; and a small, rural system, York, Nebraska. In 1962 selected units were introduced into nineteen classrooms in grades one, four, seven, and ten. To measure the effectiveness of the sequence which Nebraska was trying to incorporate into its curriculum, the systems cooperating with the Study Center introduced lessons in 1963 into grades one and two, four and five, seven and eight, and ten and eleven. By 1964 curriculum units were being taught in every grade and by 1965 teachers were working with students who had been exposed to three consecutive years of the Nebraska program. Both teachers and students involved in the testing of the units kept diaries in which to record their reactions to literary selections, theme assignments, classroom activities, and teaching techniques. Those who used the diaries to help direct the process of revision during the summer of 1963 could read with pleasure such enthusiastic comments by tenth grade students as, "This is the most exciting of the classes that I have all day because it is so different" and "I never really thought about all the things we do automatically just to utter one little word."

In the summers of 1963 and 1964, before Title XI of the expanded National Defense Education Act made funds available for institutes for teachers of English, the Nebraska Study Center, with help from the Woods Fund, the University of Nebraska faculty and administration, and school teachers and administrators, conducted workshops to revise existing materials being tested in the schools and to provide inservice training for teachers in Nebraska who might be using the Nebraska curriculum materials without having a sufficiently strong background in English or an understanding of the goals of an articulated, sequential, cumulative, spiral curriculum. Veterans of the first years of the Project returned to the University campus to act as catalysts, as seed members of small groups of teachers learning to use materials and becoming familiar with descriptive linguistics, modern rhetorics, and literary theory. Nebraska received federal funds for summer institutes for teachers in 1965, 1966, 1967, and 1968. Each summer, teachers from across the United States have come to Nebraska to study the Nebraska materials and to contribute in workshops to the continuing process of revision of the curriculum units. One might have suspected that by 1966, five years after the first burst of energy among Nebraska teachers of English, the impetus for further experimentation would have been dissipated; nothing could have been farther from the truth. Nebraska took three additional steps to improve the teaching and learning of English that year. The department of English first made application for and received funds to establish an Experienced Teacher Fellowship Program to improve the qualifications of teachers selected from throughout the United States by providing a year-long program of subject-matter courses in English and an introduction to the Nebraska curriculum materials which included the opportunity to evaluate the use of Nebraska units in schools in and around Lincoln and Omaha. The department further established a Prospective Teacher Fellowship Program and, in addition, proposed to the Office of Education a special conference on inservice training for teachers in the elementary schools.

From February 26 through March 1, 1966, fifty-eight distinguished professors and teachers from a variety of disciplines debated the issues involved in retraining teachers of grades one through six as scholars and teachers of the English language and its resources. Paul Olson, who provided the leadership for the conference, noted the rapidly changing elementary curriculum, the paucity of proposals for institutes for elementary teachers under NDEA, and the research which was clearly needed in the area of inservice curriculums for teachers in the elementary grades. In *The Arts of Language,* the official report of the Conference, Professor Olson observed, "If the conference came to a single view of the arts of language, it was, I think, that what is worth teaching teachers about is what is formed and systematic in language: in ordinary language, dialectal language, literary language or whatever—that is, the structure of rules, usages, resources which make speaking together possible. And what is systematic was thought to imply its own system of pedagogy, both for teachers and for the students of teachers; and here, obviously, we were influenced by conventional and widely known studies in the psychology of learning by Piaget, Bruner, Hunt, Carroll, and so forth." [26] Olson continued, "The group endeavored to recommend an institute policy which would bring together the distinguished and divided worlds of 'subject matter' scholar, teacher-education and curriculum scholar, classroom and school system scholar and elementary school child—perhaps to the same degree as these worlds had been brought together in the careers of the conference participants." Finally, Olson described the three central blocks of the ideal institute envisioned by the participants: language as a system, the interaction between the individual child and his society in the learning of linguistic systems and their uses, and the imaginative and discursive uses of language for children and adults.

The Conference, which provided a model for elementary institutes in 1967 and 1968 and, more important, directed the attention of the English profession to the needs of the elementary teacher, was again the product of a college department of English. The department at Nebraska, knowledgeable about the sources of funding, experienced in working with curriculum design and teacher preparation programs, prestigious enough to command the interest of such professional leaders as Albert Kitzhaber, Robert Allen, John Carroll, Raven McDavid, Owen Thomas, and William Iverson, was fulfilling its educational responsibilities to the schools of Nebraska and of the nation without compromising either the quality of its undergraduate instruction or of its graduate programs in English. Indeed, Nebraska's interest in curriculum and in the schools has led to the establishment of a new program in English Education which married the thorough knowledge of the subject of English and of research design with the opportunity to exercise influence on schools through curriculum change and research into the teaching and learning of English in the schools. Initiated in February of 1964, the program for the Ph.D. in English Education has attracted students from all over the United States to the Nebraska campus.

The Conference also sparked the Tri-University Project which Nebraska administers. The Office of Education is providing support for the University of Nebraska, New York University, and the University of Washington to participate in a cooperative program during the 1967–1968 academic year to focus national attention on the development of elementary school programs which will meet the needs of children in today's and tomorrow's schools. For the first time, three university staffs, college teachers of teachers, and elementary teachers will have worked together on the problems of elementary education. A total of thirty-seven college professors and eighty-five elementary teachers are involved in these institutes for advanced study. The college professors who are taking part were all nominated by presidents of colleges and universities which regularly graduate a large number of elementary teachers. Administered by Professor Gene Hardy at Nebraska, the Project also called an influential national conference on elementary education in February 1968.

Paul Olson outlined six major objectives for the year-long institute at Nebraska in which twelve college teachers from seven states and thirteen elementary teachers from eight states are taking part:

1. To promote and coordinate research concerning English and its learning;
2. To develop programs of scholarship and vocation for educating personnel who train teachers and to work out some meaningful programs for the involvement of English departments in the training of elementary teachers;
3. To develop training programs for elementary teachers;
4. To develop classroom materials which will permit English to be taught more effectively;
5. To demonstrate the new materials in public school classrooms; and
6. To improve college teachers as college teachers.[27]

While new projects continued to be established at Nebraska, the Study Center materials were becoming widely known as a result of their distribution to summer institutes from 1965 through 1967 by the English Institute Materials Center and through Nebraska's own efforts to mimeograph selected units requested by teachers and curriculum planners throughout the United States.

In 1967 the University of Nebraska Press, with funds allocated by the University, began to publish the Nebraska curriculum guides. Obviously the University will recover its investment, but the willingness to make the materials widely and inexpensively available by advancing a large sum of money to the Press demonstrated once again the commitment of the University of Nebraska to the improvement of the teaching of English in the American elementary and secondary school. Nebraska materials are currently being used in school systems in all fifty states, in the American Dependent Schools in Austria, England, France, Germany, Greece, Japan, the Netherlands, and Spain. Selected units are also being used by teachers in Australia, Ceylon, New Zealand, Guam, Turkey, and Colombia. In Columbus, Nebraska, a community of 12,500 citizens only fifty miles from the University, the senior high school, junior high, and seven elementary schools began teaching the entire Nebraska curriculum in the fall of 1967. Omaha Westside District Number 66 has also adopted the Nebraska program in twelve elementary schools, two junior high schools, and its senior high. In Lincoln, thirty-three elementary schools, eight junior highs, and all of the public senior high schools are teaching the Nebraska curriculum. The Nebraska school system has become, in fact, the largest and most impressive demonstration program for an experimental curriculum in America today. Visitors from all over the United States and from abroad arrive daily to observe classes, to talk with teachers and students in pilot schools, and to meet with the Study Center staff at the University.

The Nebraska Council for Educational Television has also introduced the Nebraska materials to isolated schools across Nebraska. In 1967 Esther Montgomery taught sixty lessons from the eleventh grade American literature sequence to students in 223 Nebraska schools; the number should exceed 300 in the fall of 1968. Miss Montgomery is also conducting inservice programs on television each month for Nebraska teachers who are using the Study Center materials. The Nebraska Council, moreover, initiated an inservice program to acquaint teachers with the Nebraska curriculum in the summer of 1967 by commissioning fifteen half-hour telecasts on language and composition. While at least three of the telecasts will be addressed to teachers at all levels, others will be particularly directed to elementary, to junior high, or to senior high school teachers. Teams of teachers from the state and university faculty members wrote scripts for the telecasts and prepared lessons for the American literature sequence in special workshops held in Lincoln during the summer of 1967.

No one can foresee Nebraska's future achievements in English. One can, however, predict that the experiences of the past seven years will strengthen the English curriculum in Nebraska's schools and the commitment to excellence on the part of Nebraska teachers of English. The department of English at the University, with its demonstrated ability to blend scholarly and pedagogical interests, has shown how effective a role academicians can play in school programs. Only a very few departments—at Oregon, perhaps, or at Carnegie-Mellon—can point to similar involvement. Nebraska's achievement demonstrates that a college department of English can have a significant, immediate effect on the teaching of English at all levels in its state and in the nation without sacrificing its traditional obligations to provide quality undergraduate instruction, substantive graduate programs, and inventive curriculum planning for itself as well as for the schools it serves. An Experienced Teacher Fellowship Program, a Prospective Teacher Fellowship Program, and summer institutes attract students to graduate education in growing numbers. One need only note the number of Master of Arts degrees and Ph.D.'s in English at the University between 1956 and 1967 to see how graduate programs at Nebraska have grown:

	Ph.D.	M.A.
1956–1957	0	2
1957–1958	0	7
1958–1959	Not Available	Not available
1959–1960	1	7
1960–1961	1	12
1961–1962	4	12
1962–1963	1	15
1963–1964	2	24
1964–1965	8	16
1965–1966	7	21
1966–1967	11	25[28]

An interest in the problems of the schools does not lead a department of English to lose its prestige or force it to neglect its traditional programs in British and American literature. The interest generates, rather, stronger programs at the graduate level and establishes closer ties with other departments within the university—and not only Education. Intellectual excitement in a college department is more likely to be the result of wide interests in research and teaching than of a limited commitment to traditional literary scholarship. If the college departments of English as a group need to learn one lesson from Nebraska and the few other departments in the country which have shared Nebraska's interests, it is that college professors of English must expand tremendously the range of their interests and develop a social conscience which leads to involvement with the public schools of the United States. The traditionally oriented research professor of English has an important place on any college faculty, but the perquisites and departmental rewards which have been so much his must be equally shared with those devoted to the improvement of public education in English.

No matter how thoughtfully it has been developed and how carefully it has been tested, no curriculum in English is ever finished or entirely satisfactory. At its best a curriculum proves a valuable aid to the English teacher at the same time that it stimulates questions about goals for the English program in the schools. Nebraska's design for a sequential curriculum from kindergarten through the freshman year of college, although a model of careful curriculum planning, does not lay to rest all questions about the English curriculum. Each of the major Study Centers has, in fact, provided a rationale for the curriculum it has designed. An examination of some of these overviews and a study of some of the published and unpublished reports of the Dartmouth Seminar will help outline the probable direction of curriculum planning in the 1970's.

The Carnegie-Mellon Curriculum
Robert Shafer was able to review the work of the Center at Carnegie-Mellon because he had access to the impressive materials in language, literature, and composition and to the cur-

riculum overview prepared by four members of the Carnegie staff. Like most of the Centers, Carnegie chose to design an English program for only part of the school experience, grades ten through twelve. Its first efforts to design an integrated program in language, literature, and composition for able, college-bound students led to the revision of materials to make them suitable for youngsters of average ability. The Center stated clearly that its goals included developing in the student the ability "to read with understanding and sensitivity," to have a "growing mastery of writing skills" which emerge from a composition program set up "in ordered sequential steps," and to understand "the structure, the history, and the power of the English language," again through "a sequential program" consonant with contemporary studies in linguistics.[29] The Center expressed its intention to "interrelate the programs in literature, composition, and language into a cumulative three-year sequence," in part to "contribute toward defining a standard for high school English which colleges may consider in designing their freshman courses so that learning may continue to be sequential and cumulative." Carnegie's attempt to relate the activities of the Study Center to the college department of English both by involving scholars in the production of the curriculum and by influencing the college curriculum itself is exemplary.

The Center staff agreed "that the core of the program should be the literature—that the way to develop each course was to build its literary core first and then to organize the study of composition and language around that literary core." And it developed a working definition of literature as "mankind's record, expressed in verbal art forms, of what it is like to be alive." In the tenth grade the examination of literature concentrates upon such universal human concerns as love, heroism, human weakness, and the search for wisdom. The eleventh grade course introduces American literature which shows how universal concerns are modified by the American culture pattern from Puritan times to the present. The twelfth grade student concentrates upon literary art forms, genres, and techniques. While world literature in translation has primary emphasis in tenth grade, American literature predominates in eleventh and English literature in twelfth. The composition program moves from narrowing a subject to a manageable topic and finding pertinent data to support it to communicating ideas in effective and appropriate language and, finally, to modifying the message according to the needs of the reader. The three-year language program, of course, is similarly cumulative and moves from a study of the structure of the language to semantics and to rhetoric or the effective use of language and the history of the language. The linguistic approach is structural rather than transformational-generative.

Each of the published volumes of the Carnegie materials emphasizes the importance of inductive teaching in an introductory essay on "The Inductive Teaching of English." Pointing out that some teachers "tend to think of the English class primarily as a place in which the teacher as authority imparts a body of information" (the typical college pattern), the essay urges teachers to "think of the English class primarily as a place in which the students discover knowledge and skills" as the teacher provides them with structured situations "in which, through conscious interaction with the teacher, they master the skills of English." The essay traces the honorable history of both kinds of teaching, but uses the writings of William James, Jean Piaget, and Jerome Bruner to support the observation that from "its earliest days modern psychology has tended to favor the inductive method." Detailed, day-by-day assignments and suggestions are given to help the teacher become "neither preacher nor lecturer, but guide, discussion leader, arbiter, and perhaps occasionally, resource person." The essay recommends that a teacher follow the lesson plans closely the first time he teaches the curriculum. While highly-structured lessons would seem antithetical to genuine inductive teaching, the Carnegie staff notes that the teacher cannot introduce the lessons flexibly until he has mastered techniques which promote discovery in the English classroom. His first experience with the Carnegie curriculum, then, is as much an introduction to new materials and methods for the teacher as for the pupil.

The Oregon Curriculum

The Study Center at the University of Oregon, under the direction of Albert Kitzhaber, set about to design a course of study for grades seven through twelve which included language, literature, written composition, and speech. The curriculum was conceived broadly enough "to accommodate the needs and take account of the limitations of the great majority of students—all, it is hoped, except the slowest, those for whom educational provisions of a different kind must be made." [30] To assist teachers using the Oregon materials and to inform the profession about the work of the Center, the Oregon staff prepared perhaps the most cogent and perceptive "Descriptive Essays" offered by any of the Study Centers. The overview of the Oregon materials justified changes in the English curriculum on three principal grounds. "First, textbooks, curriculum guides, and English teachers themselves have shown much uncertainty about the proper limits and purposes of English as a school subject." "Second, the existing curriculum shows a lack of sequence that has made orderly learning difficult, sometimes impossible." "Finally, much of the material in the existing curriculum is out of date, reflecting little or no awareness of the present state of knowledge in such relevant disciplines as linguistics, semantics, rhetoric, literary analysis and criticism, and the psychology of learning." Like Nebraska and Carnegie, Oregon developed a curriculum which would "improve students' control of the skills of communication" and "give students command of a body of subject matter." The Center staff argued that the subject matter it presents is not only "worth studying for the discipline that it enforces on the mind and for the knowledge that it imparts," but also "contributes toward a mastery of the skills of language." Recognizing that any sequence in English composition, for example, "is not of the same kind as in science and mathematics," Kitzhaber and his associates nonetheless assumed as had Paul Olson and his staff at Nebraska and Erwin Steinberg and the Carnegie staff, that a defensible English curriculum could be discovered which would "greatly facilitate both teaching and learning."

Having defined literature as "a record of the most thoughtful and perceptive men of all ages," the Oregon curriculum outlines an approach "predicated on the axiom that the study of literature is a discipline—that it is a study of value in and for itself, and that it has its own laws of operation and its own vocabulary." Like Carnegie's, Oregon's curriculum has its "primary emphasis on the literature itself" so that it "can do full justice to literature and to the students." Oregon builds an integrated, sequential literature program around three major components—Subject, Form, and Point of View—which are simple enough to be grasped by young readers and offer the least distortion to the whole work, the most direct route possible to dealing with that whole, and categories which are broad enough to embrace most of the aspects of literary art yet at the same time are not so broad as to be useless. *Subject,* which suggests that "any work of literature is about something" (perhaps on several levels) and invites "generalizations from the reader," should help the student "realize that a work means as well as tells." *Form* "on all levels of literature is a verbal and artistic structuring of ideas just as the thought in a sonnet must somehow be packed into fourteen lines of iambic pentameter." With echoes from Kenneth Burke, the Oregon curriculum explains that studying form will "result in the student's being aware of the arousal and satisfaction of expectations." *Point of View,* although "traditionally taken to mean the angle of vision of the narrator," is expanded to include "various attitudes toward the subject of the work—that of the author, that of the characters, and that of the reader." The student should become aware "that effective literature is affective, that the author too has a response to his subject, and that he uses various techniques of structure and rhetoric to elicit a response from his reader." The curriculum is designed to provide students "with the skill to understand any work of literature. Thus, the test of success for the curriculum would be the students' ability to apply the tools of understanding to a work outside the curriculum." Fundamental to the Oregon program is the assumption that the curriculum "will function inductively." The overview prepared by the Oregon staff, the most careful analysis of the task faced by curriculum builders in English prepared under Project English, outlines the goals of the Oregon curriculum, anticipates objections to the program, and indicates specific works and kinds of works appropriate for the curriculum at each grade level. It justifies the study of literature in the schools "on the grounds that it is at or near the center of humane studies" which "exist as an end in themselves" and "inform our whole character—or in modern jargon . . . permanently modify our behavior patterns."

Oregon makes a convincing case for teaching language "as a discipline which is of interest to humans because it is such an important part of their existence." Thus, for example, the rules of transformational grammar "reveal how from a limited number of sentence types it is possible for native speakers of our language to recreate an infinite number of transformed sentences, sentences they have never heard before or spoken. They reveal also how it is possible for native speakers of our language, by the time they are five or six years old, to understand most sentences they may come in contact with though they may never have heard the sentence before." Grade seven concentrates on a sequence of rules, known as phrase structure rules, which explain the grammatical utterances of the language. These rules lead to kernel sentences—simple, declarative, active sentences which are the basic sentences of the language. All other sentence types are derived from the kernels by processes called transformations. A special unit also introduces various social levels of language. In grades eight and nine, the student gains a mastery of increasingly more sophisticated processes. By grade nine he is also being introduced to lexicography and the history of the language, the latter expanded considerably in grade twelve. While the preliminary findings of Donald Bateman and Frank Zidonis at Ohio State suggest that a knowledge of transformational grammar may improve a student's writing ability[31] and Nebraska's lessons on revision for the ninth grade, developed by Andrew Schiller, use transformations as one of four principal kinds of revisions which will give the student command of a wide variety of sentence patterns and types, Oregon justifies the study of language, and especially of American English, for its own sake. In its language program, the Oregon Center represents most completely Professor Miller's "academic" stage in curriculum development.

Early reviewers might not have accused the Centers of a

"bypassing of the whole program of skills development" if they had had access to Oregon's defense of its curriculum in rhetoric: "We have not seen fit to treat 'correctness' (commonly ossified into a series of sterile and groundless 'rules') as an end in itself. Rather, we have considered correctness as an adjunct to the main job of communicating a given set of ideas in as effective a way as possible."

Oregon characterizes the rhetorical act as consisting of substance, structure, and style. "Substance is concerned with exploring in a responsible and even systematic way the world of facts and ideas which form the raw content for the act of communication. Structure is concerned with how to give organization and development to the substance chosen. Style deals with how to understand and use the special, smaller qualities of language which will make the composition better." Recognizing that "Drill, in the sense of merely repeating what others have written, can never lead students to the fundamentals of composing" and that "Even the beginning writer must put things together—words, ideas, experiences, arguments—that have never been put together before," the Oregon curriculum stresses "training in invention" based upon habits of observation, discrimination, and imagination. The composition lessons include work in spoken as well as written composition in each grade. The Oregon staff also presents students with a "Usage Manual" which allows the student "to answer many of his own questions on usage" and with "samples of writing by professional writers which illustrate" the principles presented in each grade.

The Oregon curriculum does, indeed, sound formidable. The challenging, content-oriented program, however, gives the English teacher practical direction for introducing students to a body of knowledge sequentially. At no point do the Oregon materials present students with units as far beyond their abilities as the Nebraska curriculum does in some secondary units. Nebraska's spiral leads students from fables and myths into satire through units prepared for grades three, six, nine, and twelve. In a formal unit on satire for grade nine, the student is introduced to such works as George Orwell's *Animal Farm* and Leonard Wibberley's *The Mouse That Roared;* less realistically, he is asked to study Alexander Pope's *Epistle to Dr. Arbuthnot,* condescendingly called "On Lousy Writers." In its plan for the twelfth grade, which introduces formal satiric devices, Menippean satire, and the mock epic through Jonathan Swift's *Verses on the Death of Dr. Swift* and *Gulliver's Travels,* Alexander Pope's *Rape of the Lock,* and excerpts from John Dryden's *Essay on Satire,* the Nebraska Center requires too much of both the student and of the average English teacher. The preparation necessary for the teacher and the impossibility of an adolescent's having the necessary grasp of the political, social, cultural, and literary backgrounds of the Augustan period suggest that a content-oriented curriculum can become quite unrealistic. Even the "Teacher's Packet" prepared by Nebraska, with its wealth of secondary material, long lists of suggested readings, and definitions of the technical terms of satire, argues for a simplification of this unit. Only the most gifted youngster could master the material in this unit in the course of a year-long literature sequence which also includes the reading of *Hamlet,* sections of *Paradise Lost* and of the *Faerie Queene,* poems by William Wordsworth and John Keats and novels by Jane Austen, Charles Dickens, and Thomas Hardy. The Nebraska Center staff, aware of the difficulty of some portions of the literature curriculum, advises the teacher to select from the units available those most appropriate for a given group of students.

Marjorie Smiley's Gateway English program is quite different from those we have previously examined. The Hunter project, "a comprehensive literature and language arts program aimed at involving disadvantaged urban adolescents in meaningful reading experiences," introduces selections "chosen because students have found them interesting and especially relevant to the problems they themselves have to face." [32] Literature becomes a way to help students achieve "emotional independence and maturity" and to formulate satisfying "personal codes and values." Emphasizing discovery rather than memorization and simple recall, *A Family Is a Way of Feeling, Stories in Song and Verse, Who Am I,* and *Coping* form a year-long program for an estimated reading level of fifth through seventh grades; programs for grades eight and nine also seek to motivate the student to learn and to convince him that school is about real things of real value to him. The writing activities introduced by Gateway defer any emphasis on correctness "until students are expressing themselves with directness, honesty, and a real desire to communicate their ideas to others both in speech and in writing." The Gateway curriculum combines the use of recorded poems and songs with significant and relevant literary selections by such authors as e. e. cummings and Gwendolyn Brooks, handsome illustrations, and a manual for teachers which states explicitly that it is not meant "to serve as a rigid formula which must be adhered to blindly." Gateway shares with all of the major Centers a conviction that inductive teaching is essential to any successful English program and emphasizes that the personal involvement of the student is far more important than his acquisition of a body of knowledge about language and literature. Although the Gateway materials were especially developed to interest urban disadvantaged youngsters, they have been received enthusiastically by adolescents from many cultural and economic backgrounds.

Daniel Fader, too, had learned to select classroom materials "to meet the practical needs of the students rather than the more abstract needs of the subject" and had stressed saturation, "meaning the replacement, whenever possible and in whatever classroom, of customary texts and workbooks with newspapers, magazines and paper-bound books" in order "to stir the sensibility of the practical child." [33]

The Northwestern Curriculum

Northwestern University's healthy scepticism about traditional methods of teaching writing in the schools is as refreshing as Gateway's attempts to make the English class come alive for students. Under the direction of Wallace W. Douglas, the Study Center in English at Northwestern developed lessons in composition for grades seven through twelve which not only challenged popular methods of teaching students to write but questioned the philosophy which lies behind the composition textbooks, workbooks, and handbooks most widely used in American schools and colleges. The well-written essay which introduces the Northwestern materials asks probing questions about the process of composing, examines the resurgence of the discipline of rhetoric in the secondary school, and outlines a composition program which encourages the student to experiment with language. Noting that the student in a typical composition class is "asked to write a paper just because he doesn't know how to," the Northwestern essay wryly asks, "What would the teacher do if there were no students who committed errors, none whose work showed definite differences from the forms and styles of writing found in the literature anthologies that the teacher used in college?" [34] The student papers which they analyzed exhibited to the Northwestern staff "a deplorable lack of contact with the real world, a dangerous refusal to look beyond words to facts" and led Professor Douglas and his colleagues to wonder how the composition class, the teaching of writing, and writing itself could be made to seem "natural and pleasurable, the occasion and means of a satisfying (even a self-consummatory) experience instead of, as they too often still are, a chance for teaching . . . that mysterious entity known as 'good English.'" Recognizing the very real pressures upon teachers in the schools, Northwestern still called upon the English teacher "so far as conscience, schoolroom, and parents will allow" to let the child "alone to do his own experimenting with his own grammatical and stylistic patterns and transformations." The Northwestern curriculum finds the teacher's chief—perhaps his only—workable device to be "the very simple one of setting up an atmosphere in the classroom, and an attitude toward language and writing, which will encourage students to try to include, *in their writing,* some of the lively, accurate words, the complex grammatical structures, and the relatively sophisticated sentence patterns that they use more or less regularly and easily in their talking." "What a teacher must not do," the curriculum cautions, "is condemn a student if he follows the grammar of his own dialect or (as is often the case) what he imagines to be the grammar of his teacher's dialect and uses a construction that is not covered by the rules of standard English." The Northwestern writers aptly observe that "As an environment for learning or practicing the art of writing, the composition class is not merely inadequate, it is probably quite obstructive or even destructive," that the "proofreader is more at home than the creator," and that every time "we treat a composition as an occasion for teaching grammar functionally or for refining a child's usages, we undermine the child's willingness to create in writing." To improve the teaching of writing, Northwestern recommends that the student be made to "feel free enough about the act of writing so that he can express his own tone and attitude" and that composition activities lead the student to observe and report, to be "filled up," not "with 'ideas' or 'subjects'—which is the usual formula— but rather with words and constructions, details, and facts." Convinced that "a student must write and write often if he is to learn to write well" and that "a student can learn to perform some of the writing functions without doing all of them," the Northwestern curriculum outlines nine steps which all writers, amateur and professional, follow. Five "Pre-Writing Steps" include analyzing the writing assignment, searching for a paper-idea, examining one's knowledge of the selected topic, gathering information, and organizing the paper. The sixth step, writing the paper, leads to three "Post Writing Steps": revising the rough draft, copying and proof-reading, and conferring with an editor (the teacher) about the paper.

The guide to the Northwestern materials also debunks the traditional four forms of discourse (narration, description, exposition, and argumentation) on the grounds "that their criteria for classification are both ambiguous and inconsistent" and do not "provide a useful, accurate framework within which the teacher can talk about an expository paper." The curriculum outlines, instead, a typology based "on the purpose of the author, the audience to which the writing is addressed, the subject matter of the paper, the degree of objectivity of the author, or the organizational type of the paper." The writer, Northwestern suggests, can report, analyze, or evaluate information in practical, journalistic, or academic style.

Northwestern's unwillingness to accept traditional school notions about composition and its analysis of the writing process lead to curriculum units which help make the English classroom a place in which youngsters will want to write and will have something about which to write. The Northwestern *Lessons in Composition* emphasize the process of writing rather than the finished essay which is its product. By encouraging the beginning writer at any grade level to experiment with language, the units shift the focus of the composition class from correctness and the mastery of formal rhetorical devices to more personal and more creative writing. In challenging the notion that writing is an activity divorced from the real lives of most students, the Northwestern Center asks teachers to abandon the theme-a-week in favor of more frequent and more varied writing activities and to set aside their red pencils in order to encourage students to become writers and not proof-readers.

The Lessons of Dartmouth

Curriculum units on literature from the Centers at Indiana University or Purdue University and on language study from those at Northern Illinois University and the University of Minnesota suggest the direction which English programs in other parts of the country have already taken. No Study Center, however, has had as disturbing an effect on the English community as the Anglo-American Conference on the Teaching and Learning of English held at Dartmouth College in 1966. The two reports on the conference, Herbert J Muller's *The Uses of English* and John Dixon's *Growth Through English*, discuss the important, troubling issues raised at Dartmouth and the sweeping changes in the English curriculum recommended by the conferees. After four weeks of intensive discussion, the fifty participants agreed on eleven points which continue to generate national and international debate:

1. The centrality of the pupil's exploring, extending, and shaping experiences in the English classroom.
2. The urgency of developing classroom approaches stressing the vital, creative, dramatic involvement of children and young people in language experiences.
3. The importance of directing more attention to speaking and listening experiences for all pupils at all levels, particularly those experiences which involve vigorous interaction among children.

4. The wisdom of providing young people at all levels with significant opportunities for the creative uses of language: creative dramatics, imaginative writing, improvisation, role playing, and similar activities.

5. The significance of rich literary experiences in the educative process and the importance of teachers of English restudying particular selections to determine their appropriateness for readers at different levels.

6. The need to overcome the restrictiveness of rigid patterns of "grouping" or "streaming" which limit the linguistic environment in which boys and girls learn English and which tend to inhibit language development.

7. The need to negate the limiting, often stultifying, impact of examination patterns which direct attention of both teachers and pupils to aspects of English which are at best superficial and often misleading.

8. The compelling urgency of improving the conditions under which English is taught in the schools: the need for more books and libraries, for better equipment, for reasonable class size, for a classroom environment which will make good teaching possible.

9. The importance of teachers of English at all levels informing themselves about the results of pertinent scholarship and research so that their classroom approaches may be guided accordingly.

10. The need for radical reform in programs of teacher education, both preservice and inservice.

11. The importance of educating the public on what is meant by good English and what is meant by good English teaching.[35]

More than 1,000 pages of "Dartmouth Seminar Papers" and the two volumes published for the interested public and for the profession enable one to gain a balanced view of the proceedings at Dartmouth. Professor Muller, writing for the educated public, explains, "One reason I was asked to write this book was an odd qualification. I knew little about the teaching of English in the elementary and secondary schools, which was the primary concern of the seminar, and had taken only a casual interest in it. It was thought that I would therefore be uncommitted, unprejudiced."[36] He acknowledges, however, "I soon lost this possible virtue, as I found the discussions uncommonly stimulating and realized more fully the importance of the issues at stake. Although I have reported in the guise of a detached observer, I should emphasize that all these issues are highly debatable . . . and that I am not in fact uncommitted or free from bias." John Dixon, too, in the polished report he prepared for members of the profession, admitted, "It has been my aim to draw from the discussions and reports at Dartmouth such ideas as are directly relevant to my own work in class and to that of teachers I know. Inevitably the selection and the interpretation involved make this a partial report—a simpler view from a single vantage point." [37] Carefully written articles in the professional journals by such participants at Dartmouth as Albert Marckwardt, Arthur Eastman, and James E. Miller, Jr. further illuminate the course of the discussions. But the "Seminar Papers"—position papers, responses, rebuttals, and committee reports—are the best indication of the intensity with which key issues about the English program in the schools were argued.

Describing the attempts at Dartmouth to define English, "the least clearly defined subject in the curriculum," Muller applauds the fact that "the questions are being asked, more persistently than ever before" and that teachers of English were searching for a philosophy. He concludes that "the disagreements were as fruitful as the final agreements" among the participants because they "at least clarified the basic issues and the reasons why these can never be resolved for good" and "demonstrated that there is still plenty of life in the subject and in the profession." The Dartmouth participants, noting the importance of reading, writing, speaking and listening well, urged "the need of making English a more liberal, humane study," a task which "would require the reeducation of most teachers, principals, superintendents, school boards—and parents." While acknowledging that "teachers of literature had to be concerned with the problem of values" (a position defended by James Miller among others), the Conference agreed that teachers of English "should neither impose their own personal beliefs on their students nor indoctrinate them with conventional beliefs, but rather should go out of their way to offer mature students works presenting diverse visions of life, a wide range of choices that may better enable them to decide for themselves." Muller wonders, however, whether most school boards and parents "really approve of such liberality, breadth, and richness."

The Seminar reached remarkable accord in objecting to the grouping or streaming of students. That accord emphasized "the injustice being done to millions of handicapped children" and the "social as well as academic" aims of education. Muller observes that when Negroes, poor children, and the unfortunate in general are segregated in the classroom, "We all suffer." He shares with Wallace Douglas, furthermore, the conviction that it is "clearly possible to do much more to realize the advantages of variety in mixed public schools" even if it is impossible "to do away with all grouping under present conditions." [38]

Establishing sequence in the English curriculum provoked some of the most interesting debate during the four weeks. While the British looked "for the principle of order in the psychological development of the child," Americans tended to look "more to subject matter or objective principles of knowledge." Although the vigorous discussion was never really along national lines, it raised serious questions about the validity of the work of the Curriculum Study Centers in English. The Dartmouth participants agreed upon the need for more continuity in the English program, but recognized "that we do not know just how to plan it," "that we should never impose any definite program on all students alike," and "that we could not be sure just when and to what extent youngsters should be introduced to formal concepts and asked to put into words what they were learning about reading and writing and judging." Their resigned conclusion that in the search for continuity "there is no one road, but many" reinforces the importance of studying and testing the sequential curriculums designed by the major Study Centers since 1962.

Everyone agreed that "English teachers need to have a sound, conscious knowledge of the language," but the British educators, especially, were disturbed by the introduction of the new grammars into the school curriculum. Muller takes a strong personal stand on the equally controversial issue of whether or not to teach students a command of standard English: "Standard English is not just a bourgeois dialect, after all, but the most common, widespread form of English, and no education for life in a democracy can be adequate without some knowledge of it. Call the preference for it ignorant or snobbish, the fact remains that it is the language of educated people everywhere, and no person can hope to talk or write appropriately and effectively for all his purposes unless he can use it with a fair degree of naturalness and correctness. . . . Refusing to teach it to poor children would automatically condemn most of them to remaining poor and unemployed, seal the division into sheep and goats." John Dixon, on the other hand, urges that the teacher "make available a variety of situations in which, if the pupil chooses, . . . knowledge may gradually become explicit and controllable" (p. 73).

While all of the conferees agreed that literature should be a central concern of the English class, they noted "that the schools have been teaching far too much knowledge, such as names and dates." The conference accepted the notion that "the teacher should choose reading that is meaningful, interesting, and enjoyable to children," but suggested also "that he should try tactfully to improve their tastes, make them more concerned about quality, and lead them toward 'the full range of literary experience that he himself can encompass.'" James Miller directs teachers of English to "select books embodying diverse visions of life and belief about values, and then question, discuss, and explore them with the students" to lead them "to an awareness of moral complexity, ambiguity, and paradox." In his discussion of the Dartmouth Conference, Miller observes that "the study of literature as recommended by the seminar might give a better idea why a people with by far the highest standard of living in all history is not clearly the happiest people on earth." Arthur Eastman summed up the discussions on literature in an address to the directors of NDEA summer institutes in English in January 1967: " . . . I think two trends-to-be were foreshadowed at Dartmouth. One was the teaching of literature as an engaging with life; the other was the teaching of literature through the instrumentalities of linguistics." [39]

The Seminar also stressed the obligation of the teacher of English to "provide opportunities and plan situations for informal conversation and discussion, often in small groups." To combat a reliance on the lecture method or the typical class discussion with its hand-waving and attempts by students to impress the teacher rather than communicate with one another,

James Britton recommended *talk*, "the sea on which everything else floats," and James Moffett described dramatic improvisation. Envisioning the English classroom as a place for the dialogue of tutor and student and of student and student, John Dixon also endorses talk, which "enters into the whole range of human interaction," and drama, which "builds, from that interaction and talk, images of human existence" (p. 34).

In his survey of the proceedings at Dartmouth, Muller observed that the group's lofty discussions inevitably "led back to the usual practical difficulties." Although he questioned how well the college English department had been serving either the national interest or the cause of liberal education, he acknowledged that a growing number of college professors "have come to feel that only by a responsible interest in better teaching can the profession claim the national support it wants." He concluded that the British on the one hand "could be charged with slighting their practical needs as members of society," but on the other "were defending the all-important human values that are being neglected in the interests of economy and efficiency, when not sacrificed to both military and commercial interests." Seen in retrospect, the Dartmouth Conference stimulated new thinking about the English curriculum, gave new currency to and supplied new definitions for such terms as creativity and drama, and emphasized the social responsibilities of the English teacher in American society.

Achievement and Challenge

What has the past decade of investigation into the nature of the English curriculum accomplished? At least three positive gains can be noted. Perhaps most important, college professors of English and school teachers are talking with one another in ever greater numbers. In recent years that dialogue has extended beyond the boundaries of the United States until in 1968 a continuing, rewarding relationship exists among members of the British National Association for the Teaching of English, the MLA, and NCTE. The Vancouver Conference of 1967 brought together teachers from Australia, Canada, England, and the United

States to talk about the English curriculum and to learn about the teaching of English from one another.

Second, the English curriculum in the American elementary and secondary schools in the next decade will reflect the active participation of scholars in curriculum development, the achievements of the Curriculum Study Centers, and the lessons which American teachers of English only began to learn from their British colleagues at Dartmouth. Even if the role of linguistics in the school program is not yet clear, the textbooks of the 1970's will certainly incorporate transformational-generative grammar, the study of dialects, lexicography, semantics, varieties of usage, and the history of the language. Literature and composition pro grams, too, will reflect the emphases on content and sequence which have marked the work of most of the Study Centers. Through teachers' manuals and guides, more and more teachers will learn how to teach inductively. In the best schools, a wide range of audio-visual materials, talk, and drama will help to motivate students to increase their skills in and knowledge of English.

A third effect of the curriculum reform which has taken place since the Basic Issues Conferences of 1958 will be substantive changes in college English courses, especially those designed for future teachers of English. The college professor who has contributed to the improvement of the school curriculum will help to change the college curriculum as well. Modern linguistics, rhetorical systems, and current literary theory will significantly modify such courses as freshman English and the introductory literature sequence. Departments of English will inevitably offer more advanced work in language and in composition, while they explore the potential uses of television and of computer-assisted instruction.

In *Improving College Teaching*, William Arrowsmith, an outspoken critic of current emphases in college and university departments of English, urges "Innovation, experiment, reform—these are crucial, and the pity is that, apart from a few noteworthy experiments, there is so little real innovation." [40] While Martin Trow finds that the "existing curriculum, especially at the introductory level, takes very little note of the diversity of the student body in the large state universities," [41] Samuel Baskin, Allan Cartter, and others can identify many innovations already affecting the college curriculum in English and in every other discipline: the development of learning centers which promote independent study; effective television instruction; computer-assisted instruction and computer time for study and research; field experience in business, government, and social work; experimentation with classroom size and arrangement and with the academic calendar; and residence-hall instruction.[42] The practical need to provide instruction for growing numbers of students, students with varying backgrounds and abilities and a well-developed sense of their right to effective teaching, and the new curriculum patterns which have been emerging in the field of English will produce significant changes in the college English program in both the junior and senior colleges in the 1970's. It is evident, for example, that the college faculty member and administrator have become more interested in good teaching each year. In his report to the seminar for college chairmen conducted by the Association of Departments of English in 1967, John Gerber said, "The case seems to be clear that one of our great responsibilities as department chairmen is to see to it that good teaching becomes a major concern of the department. There are some departments yet, I suppose, in which the mention of teaching will lead to an instant request for the chairman's resignation. In others, however, and the number of these is growing fast, the subject will be more readily received than we may suspect." [43]

Despite a growing concern for good teaching at every level and the development of a wide range of experimental curriculums for the schools and colleges, the perfect English curriculum has not yet been discovered nor will it suddenly appear in the 1970's in the guise of programmed learning or computer-assisted instruction. In the process of replacing "life adjustment" in the English classroom with the tripod of language, literature, and composition, however, those who have been interested in improving the curriculum have already contributed to the better teaching of English in the United States. In the next stages of their research, they must find ways to incorporate into the

English curriculum the lessons of the humanitarian stage which James Miller describes. They must also play a leading role in the attempts of our society to bring the socially, culturally, and economically disadvantaged youngster and adult into the mainstream of American life. English, more than any other subject in the curriculum, holds the key to the successful acculturation of students from underprivileged homes. The past decade has demonstrated that teachers of English have found new substance in their subject. The next must demonstrate that they have also found new relevance for the teaching and learning of English.

chapter two

The Teacher of English

The Lot of the English Teacher

No curriculum is teacher-proof. In recent years the teacher—whether militant, dedicated, qualified, or scraping by—has attracted the attention of newspapers and magazines throughout the United States. The wave of public interest in education which followed Sputnik I in 1957, the propaganda which accompanied federal support for institutes to retrain teachers, and two years of labor crises between the United Federation of Teachers and school boards and administrators in major school systems have earned for the teacher a permanent place in the American public forum.

In part, the public attention which education receives is a result of the increasing share of the American public—now nearly thirty percent—directly engaged in some part of the educational enterprise. In part, this interest stems from the soaring costs of public and private education in the United States. The parent, taxed heavily for education, warned regularly about enrollment pressures on the colleges, worried about the plight of the inner-city school, informed about the "New Math" and the "New English," cannot help thinking and talking about education. The elected official and the candidate for public office discover that they must be able to suggest solutions for the problems of the schools. The educator finds, at last, a national audience, willing to listen to his recommendations, but quick to judge their practicality and to measure their effectiveness against the staggering costs of substantive improvement in the schools. Disputes which formerly concerned only a small community of scholars and teachers have become the daily fodder of journals and newspapers, the hearing rooms of Congress and of state legislatures, and the inquiring eye of television.

In the past decade the teacher in the schools has begun to change both his professional and social images. He ultimately determines how successful a school administration will be, how closely the school and the community can work together, how well the curriculum will be taught. As he organizes to improve his status in the United States, he demands the right to improve his knowledge of his subject and his teaching skills. He demands, further, the right to participate with scholars, administrators, and parents in the design and execution of school programs. This chapter will examine the teacher of English in the elementary school, secondary school, and college and university both as a member of the teaching profession and as a specialist in English or the language arts.

In the fall of 1967, with more than 57 million elementary, secondary, and college students straining the physical facilities and financial resources of the nation's schools, the United States Office of Education estimated that 171,300 additional teachers were needed to join the army of 2.6 million teachers entering the schools. At the same time American colleges and universities called for 199,138 full-time professional staff members by 1969 to join the 349,386 already on campuses! The personnel needs of the American educational system and the impressive numbers of teachers already committed to the profession contributed to the growth of a new sense of power and responsibility on the part of teachers at every level of education. For growing numbers of teachers, the labor union offered a more effective way in which to exercise that power and responsibility than the educational association. When schools were unsafe, working conditions intolerable, and salaries low, the United Federation of Teachers and the American Federation of Teachers acted while the National Education Association merely talked. Earlier strikes in city schools, flare-ups between faculty and administration at institutions such as St. John's University in 1966, and the long and honorable tradition of censure used by the American Association of University Professors could not have prepared the public for the massive demonstrations of teacher power which took place in 1967. As over 45,000 of the 55,000 public school teachers in New York City struck on September 11, 1967 and as 11,000 teachers in Detroit continued the strike they had begun the week before, journalists and jurists, politicians, educators, teachers in smaller communities, and ordinary citizens and parents weighed the legal and moral obligations of teachers to meet their classes against the rights of professionals to share in establishing the educational policies of the schools in which they teach and to improve the conditions under which they work. The focus of this chapter is not upon the confrontation between organized labor and educational administration, but upon the professionalism which entitles the school and college teacher of English to demand a voice in the educational policy of his school through a union or a professional association.

Because English is taught in virtually every school and institution of higher learning in the United States, the number of English or language arts teachers exceeds that of any other discipline. Twenty percent of the college faculty may teach in the English department. More than 125,000 secondary teachers teach English classes regularly. In addition, every elementary-school teacher who operates (as most do) in a self-contained classroom must be a teacher of English or the language arts. The English teacher of the 1960's, whether helping youngsters develop skill in their native language or introducing American English to students for whom English is a second language, deserves study both because he is part of a profession searching for new responsibilities and rights within the educational community and because he teaches a subject which represents approximately twenty-four percent of the national educational effort.[2] In light of the urgent need, especially in the large cities, to help students gain command of the skills of reading, writing, listening, and speaking, men such as Clifford F. S. Bebell, Head of the Education Department at Southern Colorado State College, who argue seriously that there be a reduction in the relative amount of time given to such content-heavy subjects as English and history,[3] will remain in the minority. The teacher of English, by liberating the imaginations of students through literary experiences and by helping to develop their linguistic abilities, is probably the greatest single force for the preservation of humanistic values in our technocratic society.

In the 1960's both professional educators and popular writers have analyzed American education and the field of English. In *Up the Down Staircase*, for example, Bel Kaufman introduced the average American to the problems of the inner-city school. Although thorough, learned studies of the Chicago public school system by Robert Havighurst and Philip Hauser exposed the same administrative thickheadedness, Miss Kaufman's book attracted the kind of public attention to teaching conditions which no scholarly report could match. Her characterization of the insensitive assistant principal obsessed with forms and regulations helps the layman understand why the teacher's share in setting school policies should have been a key subject of negotiation in the strike which interrupted the education of a million children in New York City in 1967. The apathy toward and distaste for English which her protagonist's suggestion box reveals make real to a mass audience a fundamental intellectual problem in the teaching of English today—making the English classroom a relevant and meaningful place for the student. Her picture of school and community also contributes to public understanding of the citizens who manned classrooms in neighborhood schools during the New York strike and of parents who have demanded a school administration sympathetic to the problems of the community and a greater voice in school programs.

The unionization of teachers in schools and colleges, continuing scholarly and popular interest in teachers and teaching conditions, and the growing influence of education on American life have raised the status of the teacher dramatically but increased his responsibilities to society at the same time. Twenty years ago, Jacques Barzun observed, "To the man who can dig a ditch, to the athlete who can pole-vault twenty feet in the air, to the physician who delivers a baby after hours of backbreaking struggle, the world says 'Well done' and hands him his fee. But to the man who says or writes or paints a true thing tolerably well, it hardly knows how to give praise or reward. It disputes his merit, his industry, his 'seriousness.' He is at best 'a clever fellow.' " [4] Barzun's conclusion in 1944 that "any young man who intends to teach or be a scholar had better give up his ambitions at once if he hopes to receive in any satisfactory degree what is called 'recognition,' " has proved a less valid summary of the teacher's lot with each passing year. The "recognition" which the "world" has been learning—often grudgingly—to grant to the teacher, involves much more than an escalating salary schedule. It affects teacher, parent, administrator, and society as a whole. Recognition enables the teacher to regard himself as a professional person, to improve his competence as a teacher, and to take a more active part in setting policy for both school and community. Recognition of the professional status of the teacher brings the confidence of parents. Faced with inexperienced, poorly-prepared teachers, Harlem parents have justifiably demanded a greater say in running neighborhood schools. A well-qualified and dedicated faculty gives the school administrator the opportunity and the responsibility to enlist his teachers to help strengthen school programs. Updating the curriculum, reviewing testing and grouping procedures, and improving library conditions are responsibilities which must be shared by the well-informed teacher; the administrator legitimately takes these tasks upon himself only when his teachers are not qualified or committed to participate. Government—local, state, and federal—recognizes the teacher by providing funds to encourage better preparation programs, higher standards, and better working conditions for the teacher.

In English, recognition came first to the college professor, but it did not come quickly or easily. As late as 1960, the new Ph.D. in English accepted his first appointment as an instructor in a major university for approximately $5,500.00. In 1968 he will earn nearly twice that amount and join the faculty as an assistant professor. A growing college population, the shortage of qualified college teachers of English, and federal funds for curriculum research and teacher education have enabled the college English teacher to broaden the range of his activities significantly. With higher salaries, research grants from foundations and the government, and freedom from the need to moonlight, he can undertake research in libraries around the world. If he chooses to concentrate on his teaching, as most professors of English do, he has the leisure to meet with students, to read widely, and to participate actively in the affairs of his campus. Salaries at the upper end of the schedule have risen even more rapidly than beginning salaries. Professorial appointments at $25,000.00 are no longer unusual; indeed, the $40,000.00 that once seemed possible only in business and industry is distinctly possible for professors of English in the next few years. Some colleges still maintain an aura of genteel poverty for faculty, but the limited supply of college English teachers and competition for faculty from junior and community colleges is gradually forcing them, too, to acknowledge a changing academic world.

In his splendid study of the Ph.D. in English and American Literature, to be discussed at greater length later in this chapter, Don Cameron Allen discovered that seventy-six percent of the college chairmen whom he polled found it difficult to employ Ph.D.'s.[5] The chairmen estimated that there were simply too few Ph.D.'s available and that they were becoming "too expensive." Only the chairman of one of the twenty major departments in the United States, blessed with the resources of a great research library, or the chairman of a department in the New York or San Francisco areas, favored by the attraction of metropolitan life, is spared these difficulties. Hundreds of excellent college departments spread across the country, however, find it increasingly difficult to attract faculty members from the small pool of approximately 500 new Ph.D.'s in English produced in 120 institutions in America each year. Nearly all college chairmen are now willing to appoint a staff member with an intermediate degree (89.3%) and two-thirds of the chairmen would retain him (66.9%). The need to recruit and keep qualified teachers of English leads, inevitably, to higher salaries, better working conditions, and a richer professional life for the college English teacher with or without the Ph.D.

The junior or community college, the most rapidly-expanding phenomenon on the educational scene, has only begun to identify the kind of English teacher it needs and wants. That teacher is clearly not the expatriate secondary school teacher or college professor. Recognizing the uniqueness of his role in education, organized labor and the American Association of Junior Colleges have helped him to identify himself as a junior or community college teacher. Belatedly coming to understand how important a role he will play in the future of English, the professional associations in English are now calling upon him to become a leader in his own profession.

The professional and personal status of the elementary and secondary school teacher has also improved. Labor's successful efforts to raise salaries and to ameliorate teaching conditions are most apparent. The NCTE has played a significant part in giving the teacher professional recognition as a teacher of English and in working with him to improve the teaching of English in the schools and in the colleges. In the last decade the NCTE has made recommendations on acceptable teaching loads for elementary teachers, secondary teachers, and college teachers of English. Its honor roll of secondary schools which require English teachers to meet no more than one hundred students a day in four classes, its efforts to prevent censorship in the schools, its publication of important trends and issues in the teaching of English, its work to inform administrators and school boards about the English curriculum, its conventions and state affiliate meetings all give the English teacher prestige and recognition in his school and community.

As organized labor becomes even more of a force in American education, the NCTE and the MLA must prove their vitality by representing English teachers at all levels in a responsible, creative, and effective manner. The union has already demonstrated that it can help the school teacher and the teacher of English improve the conditions under which he teaches. Over the next decade organized labor will provide a voice for growing numbers of graduate students and professors of English. One hopes that labor and the associations will work together to guarantee excellence in the teaching and learning of English. For example, college and university departments of English which prepare teachers for the schools and colleges face no more important task than the examination and revision of their teacher preparation programs. Changes in these programs, however, should come from the studies and recommendations of the profession and not from union pressures. Departments of English must maintain the right to reject as well as to encourage candidates for degrees. The graduate student no more has the *right* to a Ph.D. because he has spent a certain number of years in an institution than the faithful bank clerk has a *right* to become a bank officer. He does have the right not to be exploited by the department while he is earning his degree. The implications of this right are great for the large state universities which have relied on graduate students to teach their beginning courses. There is probably no cheaper way to man a freshman class in composition than to disguise it as an internship for prospective college teachers. While students need the experience of teaching and the financial assistance it provides, they have a right to demand that their teaching be an integral part of their educational experience. The professional associations will have failed if change in teacher preparation programs can come only from the pressures of organized labor.

The teacher of English, and especially the college professor, must learn to exercise what Representative Frank Thompson of New Jersey has called "Scholar Power" not only to work reform in English but to defend the humanities in the public forum.[6] As individuals and through their associations, teachers of English can and should have a significant effect on the future of American education. In so doing, they can help the United States set its national goals and establish its priorities. Academicians have traditionally been slow to speak out on national issues, but they must do so now if federal support for the humanities is to flourish. To remain silent is to waste the recognition which has been so long in coming to the profession.

Frank G. Jennings has demonstrated that the current educational revolution did not begin with Sputnik I.[7] However, in English the latter part of 1957 did mark the start of a period of intense interest in the English curriculum and in the preparation of teachers which can be traced through a series of major reports prepared by school teachers and professors of English working together. This community of interest, the first coming together of research scholar and practitioner, is one of the most noteworthy achievements of the English profession. It broadened the scope of curriculum possibilities in the schools by drawing upon a new expertise and awakened college departments of English to their responsibilities to the schools.

Facts and Recommendations: From "Basic Issues" to the Commission on English

Of the thirty-five basic issues posed in the *Report* of the Basic Issues Conferences of 1958, seventeen deal with the preparation of teachers of English. College professors joined their colleagues in the schools to ask not only *"How much and what kind of training should the elementary school teacher have?"* but also *"What standard qualifications in English can be established for secondary school English teachers?"* and to urge that standards be made available "to guide school administrators and principals, and to enable the public to judge the quality of the schools it pays for." Aware that many graduate schools were training "students as scholars only and then recommending them to the colleges as teachers," the group asked, *"What preparation for college teaching should the Ph.D. candidate receive?"* The question was not answered until 1967. The conferees had accepted the possibility of developing a sequential and cumulative English program which would require "much closer communication and cooperation among the teachers at various levels" and therefore asked, *"How can we achieve articulation of teaching and teacher training at all levels in English?"* Finally, the convictions that "English is a subject which requires personal involvement" and that "the intellectual liveliness and interest of the teacher are likely to be reflected in the student," led the group to inquire, *"How can opportunities be made for continued education and intellectual growth for English teachers on all levels?"* Each question on teacher preparation, articulation, and inservice education was, of course, the subject for a large-scale study. The principal goal of the *Basic Issues Report* was, in fact, to stimulate members of the profession, the associations, foundations, and the government to explore the field of English.

Before many of the issues on teacher preparation raised in the *Report* could be resolved, statistical information about the teaching of English in the United States had to be gathered and analyzed. From the information amassed for *The National Interest and the Teaching of English* in 1961, the NCTE informed the profession that "the shortage of teachers . . . shows no sign of decreasing," that "One-fourth of all elementary teachers are not college graduates," and that "Only 40 to 60 per cent of the teachers of high school English have completed college majors in English." The "Standard of Preparation to Teach English" presented in *The National Interest* reflected not only the need for "more teachers, but, especially, more *highly qualified* teachers. To bring unity to a subject as complex as English, a teacher must be carefully prepared." [8] If, as G. K. Hodenfield and T. M. Stinnett wrote in the same year, "Nothing is so basic, so vital, in the education of American youth as English," [9] then *The National Interest* could only be the opening salvo in the attack on institutions with inadequate preparation programs, state certification laws which permitted the employment of unqualified teachers, and school administrators willing to allow coaches and history teachers to conduct English classes.

In perhaps the most stinging attack on teacher preparation programs in the early 1960's, James Koerner observed that the "academic departments must accept major responsibility both for the present state of teacher education and for effecting some improvements. Let it be said also that it is the academic departments that have created the educational environment in which the field of professional Education has thrived so mightily. After all, many of the failings of Education are merely aggravated copies of the failings of higher education—low standards, poor teaching, hucksterism, the proliferation of courses, empire building." [10]

The Council's campaign to improve the teaching of English continued in 1964 with *The National Interest and the Continuing Education of Teachers of English* which established incontrovertibly the central place of English in the school curriculum: "According to official records of the United States Office of

Education, 24 per cent of the total instructional time in kindergarten through grade 12 is spent on some form of instruction in English and the language arts, more than in any other subject area. In the elementary schools, where even greater stress is placed on teaching basic language skills central to virtually all learning, the percentage totals as much as 40 to 50 per cent" (pp. 4, 5). Despite the magnitude and obvious importance of English as a classroom subject, the NCTE reported that "the average elementary teacher" in its survey of more than 3,000 teachers "has devoted less than 8 per cent of his college work to English" and that fewer than "20 per cent of all elementary teachers completed a college major in English or related subjects." The study also indicated that "Almost half (49.5 per cent) of all secondary teachers who conduct English classes lack majors in the subject." In addition, it documented widespread inadequacies in inservice education programs, supervision, and instructional leadership. The alarming statistics uncovered by the two NCTE studies led the Council to prepare detailed recommendations for the preparation of teachers of English. The statistics also convinced the Office of Education and the educational community at large that massive support for the improvement of English teaching was essential to the health of the American school system.

Thoughtful critics of higher education in the 1960's have approached the complicated relationships between administration and faculty, student and professor, scholar and teacher with varying degrees of caution. In *The Profane Comedy: American Higher Education in the Sixties* (1962), Kenneth Eble of the University of Utah was seriously worried that "persisting problems" might lead to an increase in *"research* in higher education." "In English," he wrote, "one of the more verbose educational research areas, there is already a ton or more of such research that no one can read, much less make use of" and warned that "the only thing that the university need do now to make it even more incapable of solving its persistent problems is to embark on a massive research program into its own continued unwillingness to do the things it has long known need to be done" (p. 168). Harold W. Dodds, in the same year, acknowledged the entrenched conservatism of college professors even in his refutation of those deans who believe that "significant innovations toward progress habitually originate with the administration" rather than with the faculty. Charles Muscatine, on the other hand, has stated more recently that "Ninety percent of what is wrong with the modern American university is the responsibility not of the administration but of the faculty." "Any university that can get its faculty to be *scholars in regard to the university itself,*" he has observed, "will be well on the way to surviving as a university." [11]

No critic of the educational system has had more impact on the schools and on public opinion in the years since Sputnik I, however, than James B. Conant. In *The American High School Today* (1959) he gloomily noted that in "all but a few of the schools I have visited, the majority of bright boys and girls were not working hard enough." [12] Emphasizing the importance of English, he recommended "four years of English" for graduation from secondary school and specified an English program in which the "time devoted to English composition . . . should occupy about half the total time devoted to the study of English. Each student should be required to write an average of one theme a week. Themes should be corrected by the teacher. In order that teachers of English have adequate time for handling these themes, no English teacher should be responsible for more than one hundred pupils." He also recommended that those "in the ninth grade of the school who read at a level of the sixth grade or below" should receive special instruction in English from "special teachers." Although one might quibble with his directive for "one theme a week," we can only applaud Conant's concern for excellence in the English classroom. Effective teaching depends on qualified teachers with reasonable teaching loads and adequate preparation time. It is a sorry fact, as the NCTE statistics show, that in 1959 the ordinary secondary school teacher of English would not have been equipped to teach so much composition effectively. Even in 1968 he is probably not prepared to teach composition well, much less the "new linguistics" introduced into the schools in the textbooks of Paul Roberts and others. Nor is his colleague in the American college.

Five of the eighteen recommendations presented by James R. Squire in *High School Departments of English* late in 1964 have specific application to the improvement of the English teacher. Outlining the responsibilities of the chairman of a high school department of English, Squire stressed the obligation to "assess the needs of teachers for inservice courses, institutes, and workshops; advise and counsel teachers concerning course selection; and work with college or district authorities to make such offerings available." [13] He encouraged "the English faculty to cooperate with local teacher education institutions in providing varied and necessary field experience for student teachers" and to participate "in conferences designed to bring together high school and college teachers of English, articulation conferences sponsored by universities, meetings and institutes planned by NCTE and its affiliates, and the advanced placement conference of the College Entrance Examination Board." The report, like almost every piece of substantive work in English done since 1958, stressed the importance of well-prepared teachers and the need to provide inservice work by bringing together schools and colleges. No revision of the curriculum can hope to be successful if the teacher does not know enough to incorporate new material into his program.

College departments of English have generally been more alert to the needs of the secondary school teachers Professor Squire describes than to the more serious deficiencies of the elementary teacher. Eldonna L. Evertts, in *New Directions in Elementary English*, noted that "too often the elementary teacher still tries to separate the language arts and to teach the skills of each area independently." To "prepare children for the enjoyment of literature and written communication," she continued, teachers "must begin with oral language and continue to parallel the oral and the written." [14] Where the elementary school teacher will learn enough about literature for children and about the child's use of language is obviously an important question. Few college English departments could present evidence that they have even considered the special needs of the elementary teacher much less provided courses to meet those needs.

Two direct, influential antecedents of the English Teacher

Preparation Study remain to be mentioned. In 1965 the Commission on English, with Harold Martin as Chairman, published *Freedom and Discipline in English*. The report, the culmination of the work begun by the Commission in 1959 "to improve the teaching of English in America's schools and colleges," spelled out a rigorous, if traditional, program for teacher preparation aimed at the secondary teacher of "college preparatory students" but hopefully "intended to influence all tracks and all levels." [15] It reminded the public that "too much work is ordinarily required of teachers from whom, at the same time, too little professional preparation is expected" and wryly termed English teaching "not a profession but a predicament." It recommended "formal study of the history and structure of the English language," "study in rhetoric and composition above the level of the freshman course," "work in critical theory and practice with attention to bibliography and library resources," "at least one course in speech and the oral interpretation of literature," "two semester courses in American literature," "four semester courses in English literature, of which one should be the study of a single writer (preferably Shakespeare) in depth, and of which others should represent approaches not exclusively historical," "at least one course in English social and cultural history," and "enough study of one foreign language to guarantee reading facility." In addition to subject matter requirements, it outlined a course of study in pedagogical processes which would include the following: "one course in the psychology of learning, one course in the methodology of the subject (selection of materials, lesson planning, curriculum development, review of relevant research), one course in the history of American educational theory and institutions," and "one semester of full-time practice teaching under close and competent supervision." Sometimes reading more like a program for the college English teacher than for the school teacher of English, the report has been attacked for its blandness, conservatism, and timidity, but it did draw wide attention to the belief that "clear standards of preparation, if instituted and enforced, would guarantee a distinct improvement in the quantity and quality of knowledge purveyed in the classroom and, one can reasonably assume, in the mastery of the skills taught there."

Reviewing *Freedom and Discipline,* however, Wallace Douglas reflected the distress with which some members of the profession greeted the conservative report, as a document which did not seem to have progressed beyond the *Basic Issues Report* of 1959 and one which ignored almost completely the great social revolution which was taking place in the United States. Douglas sadly noted "elegant evidence of the enormous power of resistance in the ideology of English teachers" and "a balancing of old and new to the end of constructing a palatable consensus that will suggest the presence of thought but will in no sense require any fundamental change." Early in 1966 the Curriculum Commission of the NCTE, perhaps reacting to the academic orientation of *Freedom and Discipline,* admitted in *Ends and Issues* that there was "confusion about the English curriculum" arising "out of a massive movement to reshape American education," a movement which required the English profession to ask, "Have recent developments for academically talented students crowded out attention to the mass of students without academic aspirations?" The answer was clearly "Yes."

The twenty pilot institutes for teachers organized by the Commission on English in 1962 are probably a far more important contribution to the improvement of teacher preparation programs than *Freedom and Discipline.* As John Gerber of the University of Iowa reported in his evaluation of the institutes, "What makes these Institutes of especial significance . . . is that the program required twenty of the most influential Departments of English in the country to involve themselves directly in this advanced training of high-school teachers. These were . . . institutes administered and largely taught by professors of English." [17] Moreover, the institute pattern which was developed by the twenty departments became the model for many of the federally supported institutes for teachers of English in 1965. Without the model of the Institutes of the Commission on English, it would have been impossible for many departments of English so promptly to submit proposals to the Office of Education and to interest college professors of English in working with high school teachers. The patterns have changed summer by summer, but the profession owes an incalculable debt to the Commission for its contribution to the successes of the first summer of NDEA.

NCTE Leads the Way

The fifth volume of the NCTE Curriculum Series, *The Education of Teachers of English for American Schools and Colleges* (1963), edited by Alfred H. Grommon, presents the recommendations of the thirty-three nationally known teachers and scholars who then constituted the NCTE Commission on the English Curriculum. Concerned with the pre-service and inservice preparation of teachers of English at all levels, the volume was the most comprehensive, detailed report on the teacher of English which had ever been presented to the profession. Two of its great strengths lay in its emphasis on continuing education and in its discussion of the education of college teachers. The recommendations of the Curriculum Commission provided the cornerstone for the English Teacher Preparation Study, in which the NCTE and the MLA joined with the National Association of State Directors of Teacher Education and Certification (NASDTEC) to change certification requirements for teachers of English, helped prepare the profession to accept the recommendations on the Ph.D. in English which resulted from the MLA study conducted by Don Cameron Allen in 1966–1967, and established an interest in teacher education which has since led to a study of the preparation of teachers for junior and community colleges by the MLA, NCTE, and American Association of Junior Colleges and to a series of recommendations on doctoral programs in English Education prepared under the thoughtful direction of Dwight Burton of Florida State University. Professor Grommon, whose role in making the English profession aware of its responsibility to prepare qualified teachers at every level cannot be overestimated, noted in 1963 that "Professional education and academic groups . . . are studying with renewed energy problems of teachers' qualifications, preparation, and certification; examining the demands created by universal education in a democratic society; and experimenting with means of securing enough qualified teachers to meet the continuing increase in enrollments throughout the education system." He identified five major goals which effective teacher preparation programs should help the preparing teacher reach:

> First, all young people, to the highest degree possible, should discover in the English language an effective instrument of thought, expression, and communication.
>
> Second, the student should learn to use language "not merely as a medium of communicating but also for expression of one's own thoughts and feelings."
>
> Third, a candidate for teaching should cultivate "reading for personal values and social insight."
>
> Fourth, a prospective teacher should develop intelligent, critical, and appreciative use of the mass media of communication.
>
> Fifth, a teacher should be prepared to help his students find in English a significant general education that is the right of all and is also the important component of vocational education.[18]

The volume is, of course, essential reading for anyone seriously interested in the preparation of teachers of English, as is Professor Grommon's authoritative history of teacher preparation in English in the United States (*English Journal*, April 1968). Although the thoroughness of the Commission's report and its scope make summaries of the recommendations difficult, a selection of major ideas will demonstrate how greatly the study influenced the English Teacher Preparation Study. In addition to urging high standards of selection and evaluation of prospective teachers at all levels and asking the English department to take part in the selection and evaluation rather than leaving these important matters entirely to departments and colleges of education, the report outlined a program for the elementary teacher which "should include a relatively equal emphasis upon (1) general education, (2) professional education, and (3) an academic field of concentration"—perhaps but not necessarily the language arts. As a minimum requirement the elementary teacher should have taken "at least one course in advanced composition beyond freshman English; one in the historical development, structure, and social functions of the English language, taught with the non-major student in mind; and two in literature, one covering major writers or masterpieces of American Literature and one in English or world masterpieces." Institutions were urged to move "as rapidly as possible toward five-year programs planned as a unified and well-articulated sequence in both academic and professional work" (pp. 18–19). Work in composition and in language to complement the study of literature was an additional, important emphasis.

The secondary teacher, who has frequently received greater attention than the teacher at other levels, was asked to give "at least 40 per cent of his study to general education, at least 40 per cent to academic specialization, no more than 20 per cent to professional preparation," and to present a "major or minor in English" which included "at least one course in composition beyond the freshman year, courses in the history of the language and in modern grammar, and training in public speaking, in addition to a balanced program in literature" (p. 144).

The chapters on "The Undergraduate Education of the Future Teacher of College English" (pp. 513–536) and on "The Doctoral Program for the Teacher of College English" (pp. 539–563) emphasized not only the usual call for a strong and balanced graduate program, but a new willingness on the part of college teachers of English to set their own house in order. Warner G. Rice challenged the establishment most directly in "How the Candidate Learns To Teach College English": "If, then, departments of English think that college teaching is important, they must accept the obligation for providing a more thorough discipline in the art than they have attempted in the past" (p. 583).

They have accepted that obligation. MLA, NCTE, and the fledgling Association of Departments of English first called together fifteen chairmen, scholars, and teachers in June 1965 to draft a "Policy Statement" on the Ph.D. in English. The five resolutions of the conference spelled out a four-year graduate program which required a knowledge of one foreign language and a dissertation which was "a demonstration of scholarly and rhetorical ability." Addressing themselves to the preparation for teaching of the college professor, the conferees stated, "Employment of the doctoral candidate in instructional duties should be restricted to his useful training as a teacher and should not be prolonged beyond the point at which it ceases to serve this purpose."

The Conference on the Ph.D. in English, aware that "No

dependable statistics exist as to the shortage of college teachers of English," called for future conferences and studies to resolve at least five major questions discussed on June 15–16.[19] Although it might well reveal deficiencies as troubling as those presented in *The National Interest and the Continuing Education of Teachers of English,* a study of the graduate training of the college professor of English was clearly in order. As early as 1960 Bernard Berelson had surveyed graduate programs throughout the United States and offered nineteen recommendations in *Graduate Education in the United States,* including the call for a *"four-year doctorate," "some* actual teaching experience" for all doctoral candidates, a *"shorter"* dissertation, the elimination of the *"final oral examination,"* and a *"new* intermediate degree."[20]

With financial support from the Danforth Foundation, the MLA embarked on a study of graduate programs in English and American Literature in 1966–1967. Don Cameron Allen, Sir William Osler Professor at the Johns Hopkins University, chairman of his department, and a distinguished Renaissance scholar, agreed to direct the study and write a report on *The Ph.D. in English and American Literature* based upon five conferences involving the chairmen of the 120 departments of English in the United States and Canada which offer the doctorate and upon the results of lengthy questionnaires addressed to all those who had received the Ph.D. between 1955 and 1965, graduate professors of English, the chairmen of graduate departments of English, and a sampling of chairmen of departments not offering the Ph.D. His witty, informative book, published in the spring of 1968, informed the public that graduate training in English badly needed reform and that the profession seemed ready to undertake that reform.

Berelson had argued in 1960 that "the mere presence of criticism is not enough to warrant serious changes" in graduate programs. "Criticism," he wrote, "is endemic in the educational world and will be as long as clear measures of the quality of the product are not available—and after too, for that matter" (p. 217). Professor Allen, however, had statistical information about graduate training in English which allowed him to assess the quality of that training with authority. He noted that in English "the lack of uniformity in graduate programs is greatly surpassed by our persistent avoidance of self-criticism. The whole system brought across the Atlantic by Americans of the last century has become fossilized, and like all fossils is dead and stone cold. We have only infrequently asked ourselves what we are doing or why we are doing it. . . . In primitive societies a youth starved, stuck himself with bone needles, held fire in his hand, and after forty days had a vision from which he took his name; but it is not recorded that any of these initiates called himself 'Doctor of Philosophy in English Literature.' " [21] Allen further observed that the "best argument in favor of many graduate courses is that they instruct the student in 'how not to teach.' " Like many of his colleagues, Professor Allen was disturbed to learn that, on the average, the candidate for the Ph.D. in English would spend nearly eleven years earning his doctorate, years marked by the learning of foreign languages which would not be used in his graduate training, written examinations which might last as long as forty-eight hours, and a general indifference to the development of teaching skills. Professor Allen's survey showed that of the 1880 recipients of the degree between 1955 and 1965, 689 had spent no time at all as teaching fellows between the A.B. and the Ph.D. He learned, moreover, that despite the great emphasis which the graduate schools place upon research and publication, 40.8% of the recipients had, in fact, published nothing at all. While his survey showed, on the one hand, that 39.8% of the graduate departments were doing "nothing" to instruct doctoral candidates about their college and junior college duties, it showed, on the other, that 97% of the college chairmen in his sample felt the need for improving graduate training in English. Even though his statistics demonstrated how badly the profession needed to attract more students into graduate work and to produce a larger number of qualified Ph.D.'s each year, they showed, too, that nearly half of the chairmen of graduate departments and graduate professors felt that the proliferation of graduate departments since 1900 had had a "bad effect" upon the profession.

Even before his book was published, however, he and a small group of the most prestigious professors of English in the United

States had drafted and offered to the profession eleven recommendations for "departments now offering the Ph.D. in English"
and "those preparing to do so." [22]

Recommending that the "Ph.D. student should do a limited
amount of supervised teaching as part of his program," the
committee explained, "By limited amount is meant no more than
one class per term in the second and third years of the program.
The teaching should be supervised and should require attention
to both composition and literature. Departments should regard
teaching as part of the student's education, not as a means of
staffing courses." It was natural that the committee should address itself to so crucial an issue. As Professor Allen later observed, "The recommendation that each graduate student be
required to do practice teaching is not a commendation of the
long drawn-out teaching assistantship already denounced; it
springs from the realization that it is unfair to society to send
out pedagogically ignorant Ph.D.'s whose teaching powers are
unknown and cannot be described."

Other recommendations suggested the design for a doctoral
program which could be completed in four years of full-time
study. "The dissertation," for example, "should be of such scope
that it can be completed within twelve months of full time
work," a responsibility "of the supervisor as well as of the
candidate." The committee, after a careful analysis of the information on current graduate programs and the statistics on
the supply and demand for college English teachers collected
by Professor Allen, urged the abolition of the examination after
the dissertation, the awarding of an interim degree (such as the
Candidate in Philosophy offered at the University of Michigan
for the first time in 1967 or the Master of Philosophy awarded
at Yale) "to a student who has completed all requirements except the dissertation," and a study of "the feasibility of systematic
post-doctoral work in English." The Ph.D. which Professor Allen
and his colleagues recommend is a graduate degree with high
but realistic standards. The emphasis on teaching experience and
on a balanced program which includes language and composition
as well as literature shows an awareness that almost every Ph.D.
in English is, first of all, a college *teacher*. At its worst, the

established doctoral program in American universities assumed that every Ph.D. would become a publishing scholar. Professor Allen proved that this is not the case.

The encrustations which had grown up around the Ph.D. in many departments are being chipped away in universities like Johns Hopkins, Indiana, New Mexico, and Oregon. The Allen report, recommended by its common sense and by the enormous prestige of those involved, has already speeded up the process. Professor Allen discovered early in his study that most chairmen of graduate departments of English were eager to reexamine their doctoral programs. In retrospect, it seems that the profession had waited a decade for his study.

Among the reports, studies, and conferences which have influenced teacher preparation, the Anglo-American Conference on the Teaching of English held at Dartmouth College in 1966 deserves special mention. The presence of British educators and four uninterrupted weeks of discussion enabled many American scholars and teachers to clarify their notions not only about English as a school subject but about the background and qualifications of the ideal teacher of English.

In *The Disappearing Dais* (1966) Frank Whitehead, one of the most outspoken of the English participants at Dartmouth, presented a view of English which met with the sympathies of the fifty conferees: "English, then, is central to the child's all-round growth towards maturity and its true objectives can be achieved only when his whole personality is involved, on a more than superficial level, in the activities of the English lesson." [23] In English, therefore, "even more than in any other subject, it is a *sine qua non* for the teacher that he should understand his pupils in depth, sympathise with their needs and aspirations, and be perceptively aware of their individual rhythms of growth and development." As noted earlier, Dartmouth did not ignore the knowledge of his field which an English teacher must possess, but it emphasized the teacher's need to understand "that every child is a unique individual" and to stimulate the child's "strong motivation and keen interest."

Another participant at Dartmouth, David Holbrook, had affirmed the same principle in *English for the Rejected* (1964) by presenting six guidelines for teachers working with urban disadvantaged youngsters: *Strive not only to see the children as human creatures of great value, but treat them as such; Always be flexible and spontaneous; Don't expect any but the slightest and most intangible of results; Be prepared to jump for joy at the least success, and show it;* [Have] *endless and unflagging encouragement;* and, finally, *Do not bother overmuch about spelling and punctuation in creative work.*[24] Both Holbrook and Whitehead emphasize the human values in teaching rather than the communication of any body of knowledge about English.

The Dartmouth Seminar discussion of teacher preparation focused less on changes in the content of programs in teacher education than on change in *attitudes* toward such programs, and a recognition of the social, professional, and educational context in which such teacher education must occur. "Especially important," Dartmouth noted, is "the relationship between the work of the colleges and universities and the reality of the classroom in the field." The seminar members argued that the "processes through which the teacher of English is himself prepared to teach must be compatible to some degree with the processes which he will introduce in his own classrooms" and not an "unimaginative, routinized compartmentalized education . . . isolated from the larger educational scene."[25] While none of the earlier reports of recommendations had envisioned a teacher education program which ignored the child as a responsive individual, Dartmouth spoke out most vigorously for committed, creative teachers of English.

The *Report* of the Basic Issues Conferences, the *National Interest* studies, the NCTE annual bibliography on *The Preparation and Certification of Teachers of English* (edited since 1957 by Autrey Nell Wiley), the Dartmouth Seminar, the Allen report, and dozens of other studies and papers exemplified nationwide efforts, to improve the preparation of all teachers of English. At every level of education English teachers had begun to escape from complacency, to talk with one another, and to establish a national voice.

Fortunately for the profession, the National Association of State Directors of Teacher Education and Certification

(NASDTEC) had begun to work closely with the disciplines to raise certification standards in 1958. Operating within state departments of education, the NASDTEC member normally exercises the state responsibility to give legal accreditation or approval of institutions and programs for the education of teachers. Cooperating with the American Association for the Advancement of Science (AAAS), and with the support of the Carnegie Corporation of New York, NASDTEC first developed and circulated widely *Guidelines for Science and Mathematics in the Preparation Program of Elementary School Teachers* and *Guidelines for Preparation Programs of Teachers of Secondary School Science and Mathematics* in 1961. NASDTEC's "Declaration of Policy on Teacher Education and Certification" of June 24, 1958, declared that: "NASDTEC believes that the growing and changing demands on society in the last half of the twentieth century require that . . . all teachers have a broad education in the arts, the sciences and the humanities; *intensive study* in the subject matter fields to be taught; and thorough preparation in the education process." The quick acceptance of these early guidelines by more than forty states led NASDTEC to begin a second study in cooperation with the MLA, again financed by the Carnegie Corporation. The forceful leadership of F. André Paquette produced *Guidelines for Teacher Education Programs in Modern Foreign Languages* in 1966 which have already been accepted in a dozen states.

Although a national, cooperative effort to write guidelines for the preparation of teachers of English for the schools did not begin until 1965, the Cooperative Research Branch of the Office of Education had begun supporting the Illinois Statewide Curriculum Study Center in the Preparation of Secondary School English Teachers (ISCPET) in August 1964. Technically only a statewide program involving twenty colleges and universities in Illinois, ISCPET immediately established a model for statewide articulation on the preparation of teachers of English. Unlike the Minnesota pattern of centralized conferences on certification conducted by Harold Allen of the University of Minnesota and funded by the Upper Midwest Regional Educational Laboratory, J. N. Hook's ISCPET established local research programs on college and university campuses throughout Illinois. Greenville College, for example, undertook a nationwide study of the supervision of student teaching in English. Of immediate value to those who began the English Teacher Preparation Study in 1965, however, was the publication of ISCPET's preliminary statement on the "Qualifications of Secondary School Teachers." [26] To be published in a revised form in 1969, the qualifications statement is "an instrument to help English teachers measure their competencies against those suggested by national authorities in English, Speech, and Education and to assist institutions in Illinois and throughout the United States to measure the quality of their teacher preparation programs." Since 1965, more than 40,000 copies of the statement have been circulated to students and teachers in classrooms, institutes, and workshops. The document lists minimal, good, and superior qualifications in five areas: knowledge of language, knowledge and skill in written composition, knowledge and skill in literature, knowledge and skill in oral communication, and knowledge and skill in the teaching of English.

NASDTEC had shown its leadership in working with the disciplines to improve certification standards in the states. College professors of English and Education, classroom teachers from both the elementary and secondary schools, school and college administrators, and representatives from such associations as the International Reading Association (IRA) and the Association for Supervision and Curriculum Development (ASCD) had demonstrated that they could and were eager to work with one another. The Office of Education had supported programs to improve the pre- and inservice education of teachers of English through Project English or the English Program of the Office of Education and through the summer institutes for teachers authorized by Title XI of the amended NDEA.

The English Teacher Preparation Study

Accordingly, with funds from the Cooperative Research Program, the MLA, NCTE, and NASDTEC launched the eighteen-month English Teacher Preparation Study (ETPS) in September 1965 under the direction of William B. Viall, Executive Secretary of NASDTEC. The project was the culmination of the dreams and plans of many English teachers, particularly of Autrey Nell Wiley, Eugene Slaughter, and Donald Tuttle. With James R. Squire as Chairman of the Advisory Board, the staff and board met for the first time in Denver early in September. The group agreed that the guidelines would be written for the teacher of English at any level and that the final document would emerge from successive drafts presented to groups of scholars, teachers, and administrators at dozens of association meetings, at four regional conferences, and at a national conference in January 1967.

Thirty chairmen of college departments of English and of Education attending the South Central MLA meeting in New Orleans reviewed the first draft in October. Obviously heavily influenced by the ISCPET qualifications statement and by the recommendations of the NCTE and of the Commission on English, draft one was politely but sceptically received. A revised second draft, less a piecing together of previous documents and more a statement in its own right, was presented to seventy teachers and scholars in Boston in November at the first two-day regional conference on teacher preparation standards in English. As sixteen subsequent drafts were hammered out in friendly and occasionally in acrimonious debate, members of the ETPS board and staff introduced the guidelines and explained the purposes of the study to ten state meetings of teachers called by NASDTEC, to affiliate groups of NCTE, to other regional MLA meetings, and to the national conventions of the MLA, NASDTEC, NCTE, IRA, ASCD, the Conference on English Education, and the Conference on College Composition and Communication. The document was reviewed and revised on planes and in airports as well as in association conference rooms and around green, felt-covered tables in hotels in almost every state in the union in the course of the 150,000 miles traveled by the three members of the staff. Near the end of the study, Nelson Francis of Brown University dubbed the ETPS "the oldest continuous floating conference in America." While the board and staff expected the most significant revisions of the manuscript to come from the regional conferences held in Salt Lake City in January 1966, in

Iowa City in May 1966, and in Charlotte, North Carolina, in October 1966, they received hundreds of comments and revisions from the 5,800 NDEA summer institute participants who examined the guidelines and from department chairmen and specialists in English Education who had studied the drafts published in the *ADE Bulletin* and in the *CEE Newsletter.*

By January of 1967 the board was ready to present draft eighteen to the 175 teachers, scholars, and administrators invited to Chicago for the national ETPS conference. Their revisions had been especially careful in December as they combed through the marked copies of drafts and letters. If the national conference could accept the guidelines, they would be presented to NASDTEC for formal endorsement immediately following the conference and then to the Executive Council of MLA and the Executive Committee of NCTE in March.

When the snow began to fall during the night, no Chicagoan expected Thursday, January 26, 1967, to be a notable day. Even the weatherman predicted only a snowy, blustery January day typical of the Chicago winter. That morning, teachers and scholars throughout the United States packed their bags, restudied draft eighteen of the guidelines, and prepared to come to Chicago for the meeting scheduled to begin that evening. Thirty-five NASDTEC members, involved in a business meeting of their own, noticed when they broke for lunch the snow coming down harder and a snarl of traffic on State Street that signaled later trains and planes which might delay the opening of the three-day ETPS meeting. When his plane was canceled, James Squire boarded a bus in Detroit to be sure that he would arrive in Chicago in time for the meeting; he little knew that the massive drifts of snow in Gary, Indiana, would trap his bus for three days. Despite the twenty-six inches of snow which paralyzed Chicago for four days and stranded or kept at home more than half of those invited to attend the final conference, seventy-nine persons refined and polished the guidelines on Friday and Saturday. Perhaps a closer group in their isolation, they would not again experience so dramatic a finale to a study project in English.

Endorsed by the sponsoring associations, the *Guidelines for the Preparation of Teachers of English* was officially published in the journals of the MLA and NCTE early in the fall.[27] On what kind of document had so many persons labored so long? In what ways could it direct the course of teacher preparation in English for the next decade? Had the English profession taken a step beyond the earlier achievements of the NCTE and the Commission on English? Because the guidelines reflect the best thinking of the profession, they deserve careful review.

The guidelines attempt to suggest desirable competencies for teachers of English in the elementary and secondary schools. They should help State Departments of Education to evaluate programs for the preparation of teachers offered by institutions which seek accreditation and by individual applicants for certification. They are also intended to help colleges and universities develop and evaluate programs which prepare teachers and should encourage institutions of higher learning to select and recruit good teachers for the English classroom. They are not intended to be used arbitrarily in the certification process in any state, but they suggest a context within which programs for the preparation of teachers of English can be evaluated with discretion and imagination. Among the most important functions of the guidelines is to stimulate colleges to experiment with curriculum patterns which promise to improve the teaching of English. In light of the pressing need for more teachers with higher qualifications, the guidelines reinforce the responsibility of college departments of English to participate actively in the development of teacher education programs in English, together with departments of Education and Psychology and Sociology and Curriculum, to design new courses and to plan new course arrangements for English preparation programs. While growing numbers of English teachers have special responsibilities beyond the scope of the ordinary elementary or secondary classroom, the guidelines do not attempt to outline the special skills required of teachers working with preschool children, junior high school students, the urban or rural disadvantaged, or those learning English as a second language. Although the guidelines cover many areas, they rest finally on two basic assumptions true for all English teachers: to teach the content of his subject effectively, the teacher must not only have a command of the varied subject matter of English but know how to communicate his knowledge and his appreciation to students. Furthermore, his teacher preparation program must begin with a background in the liberal arts and sciences.

Those who wrote the guidelines were quite aware that not every beginning teacher of English—or retiring one, for that matter—could have mastered all the knowledge and skills described in the document. The guidelines identify the areas in which a beginning teacher must have done some studying and they suggest the direction, diversity, and depth of his future study. State certification officers, college departments of English, and school administrators must find the means to bring the individual teacher of English in the American school closer to the challenging goals expressed by the guidelines. The parent with children in school and the taxpayer supporting public education in the United States can use the guidelines to measure the quality of the English teaching in his own school and community. New buildings, more course offerings, and a welter of school activities are not effective substitutes for qualified teachers in English or in any other school subject.

Upon first inspection the guidelines seem ambitious, perhaps unrealistically so, and somewhat bland. Upon closer examination they suggest radical and necessary reforms in American colleges and universities. Some readers are puzzled by the inclusion of all elementary school teachers in a study devoted to English. The ETPS staff and board recognized that the elementary teacher must be able to teach many subjects. The study carefully avoids suggesting that the self-contained classroom be replaced by a departmentalized system, although beyond the first two or three grades such changes seem relatively certain. Still, when the guidelines refer to "the teacher of English at any level," they refer at once to the secondary teacher of English, who is a specialist in English, and to the elementary school teacher, who, despite his other professional obligations, spends 40 to 60 per cent of his time teaching English and related skills. The amount of preparation in English will, naturally, be smaller for the elementary teacher than for the secondary teacher, but teachers at both levels will need to follow a program that provides the balance and the emphases indicated in the guidelines.

Who Shall Teach English?

Two concerns govern the initial recommendation that *The teacher of English at any level should have personal qualities which will contribute to his success as a classroom teacher and should have a broad background in the liberal arts and sciences.* Without specifying how a college or university can or should choose and evaluate the prospective teacher, the guideline emphasizes that the teaching professional must be a special kind of person if he is to work with children and adolescents successfully. No department of English will have an easy time measuring the maturity, self-knowledge, sense of humor, and self-discipline of the college student who expresses an interest in teaching. It will be even more difficult to identify and to encourage the creative young person to enter teaching. Many young men and women do not enter teaching because they have been put off by their image of the pedestrian teacher or scholar and the stagnant classroom in which rote learning stifles creative imagination and individuality. The first guideline challenges talented, creative college students to enter teaching. It challenges colleges and universities to establish programs which attract such students. It asks department chairmen to involve their most distinguished teachers in teacher preparation programs. The guideline also suggests to the schools that they encourage exciting, creative teachers to experiment with new approaches and new materials for teaching English.

The second part of the guideline reasserts the well-established but often neglected notion that *every* teacher be, first of all, a rounded, cultivated, informed human being. Throughout the discussions of various drafts of the document, the value of knowing a foreign language, especially for elementary teachers, was hotly debated. The study points out that in addition to the important advantages which accrue from a practical command of any living foreign language in today's shrinking world, the increasing variety of languages and dialects spoken in American schools makes it virtually imperative that both elementary and secondary teachers be familiar with a foreign language, with the methods by which English is taught to speakers of another language or dialect, and with the psychological processes involved in learning a second language or dialect. Ideally the teacher at any level will know something about science and mathematics because they are important in the modern world. He will also have studied some subjects such as anthropology, philosophy, and the economic, political, and cultural histories of the United States and of England. Work in speech will, first of all, help the teacher to listen more critically and speak and read aloud more effectively, and second, prepare him to help his students to acquire these skills. He studies and practices the fine and applied arts because they are valuable in themselves, because they enrich his own cultural life, and because they enhance his ability as a teacher to recognize, nourish, and evaluate the creative work and artistic techniques of his students. The complaint that many teacher preparation programs, especially in elementary education, are so filled with courses in professional education that the prospective teacher does not have the opportunity to mature as an educated human being reinforces the importance of this first guideline. Let us first have educated human beings for our teachers; let us then infuse them with a knowledge of, a passion for, and the skill to teach English.

When would any student who expected to graduate in four, five, or even six years find the time to study in so many areas? The guideline deliberately does not discuss the number of hours in the humanities, social sciences, natural and biological sciences, and in the arts which the individual student should take. It does insist that the department and college should constantly reexamine programs lest the special requirements for teaching overwhelm the student's opportunities to become an educated person. These remarks should not be construed as an attack on "Education" courses *per se*. Many departments of English, in fact, are offering to their students, and particularly to prospective teachers, watered-down surveys of literature and language courses which cannot hope to stimulate intellectual curiosity and interest. Many courses in Education spoon-feed prospective teachers information which they might better learn on their own. Some fields, perhaps reading most of all, continue to extend the number of courses which they offer and require instead of reexamining periodically the intellectual value of their existing courses.

Although the second guideline stipulates particular courses and areas of emphasis, it does not infringe on the right of each state to decide what constitutes an approved program, nor does it specify the number of course hours which constitute a satisfactory preparation program in English. The entire document, in fact, carefully avoids confusing courses or hours with desirable competencies and skills. Many of those deeply involved in the study, however, agreed that at least fifteen semester hours or the equivalent in English above the level of freshman English was essential for the elementary teacher and that the secondary teacher needed a minimum of thirty-six semester hours or the equivalent above the level of freshman English.

The guideline suggests that *The program in English for the elementary school teacher should provide a balanced study of language, literature, and composition above the level of freshman English.* In addition, *the program should require supervised teaching and English or language arts methods, including the teaching of reading, and it should provide for a fifth year of study.* For the secondary school teacher of English, the program should constitute a balanced major, *supervised teaching and English methods, including the teaching of reading at the secondary level,* and a fifth-year *largely in graduate courses in English and in English Education.*

Four important points are made in the second guideline. The first is *balance* in the English program. Often the teacher of English (even at the graduate level) has taken his work almost exclusively in literature. For his own needs and for his teaching he must have advanced work in language and in oral and written composition. Guidelines three and four spell out the kinds of skills and knowledge he should find in his English courses. The elementary teacher, who may teach many subjects in a self-contained classroom, cannot hope to do more than begin a carefully balanced sequence of courses in English which he can supplement in a flexible, individually designed fifth-year program and through additional inservice courses, workshops, and institutes. Even the secondary school teacher of English, who can obtain a strong, balanced English major, will need to undertake a fifth year of study and later inservice work in order to cover the many parts of English which deserve his attention.

The second precept of this guideline is one that needs to be noted by those who are planning graduate programs in English as well as by those who are revising undergraduate teacher preparation programs. The future college teacher of English needs English methods and carefully supervised practice teaching as surely as the elementary or secondary school teacher. The recommendation that supervised teaching be included as a formal part of the graduate program in English which emerged from the Allen report on the Ph.D. must force college professors to change their shockingly condescending attitude towards methods and practice teaching. It is fallacious to assume, as many professors still do, that the college faculty member will learn to teach well—somehow. Although chairmen of departments of English indicate that salary increments and promotions are based on "good teaching," they are often hard pressed to explain how anyone knows the quality of the teaching that goes on in a department. It is true, of course, as many chairmen point out, that students evaluate the teaching in a department and share their opinions with their colleagues and with the faculty. It seems a great pity, however, that college teachers as a profession pay little more than lip-service to one of their most important continuing responsibilities—excellence in teaching.

Third, the guidelines emphasize that teachers of English need to know something about the teaching of reading. The elementary teacher, of course, works with developmental reading throughout the day, but he and the secondary teacher need also to know how to recognize reading deficiencies that should be called to the attention of reading specialists. The English teacher cannot hope to become a reading specialist, but he must be able to help every student learn to read in many ways—to read newspapers and magazines, to explore the imagery of a poem, the rhetoric of a sentence.

Fourth, this guideline stresses the flexible fifth year which may be taken prior to teaching, during summers, or through accredited extension or inservice courses taken during the school year, ordinarily to be completed within the first five years of teaching. The guideline does not insist that the fifth year be at the graduate level, or lead to a master's degree, nor, indeed, that all of the teacher's work in the fifth year be in English. The individual needs, deficiencies, and interests of the new teacher will shape his fifth-year program. For some secondary teachers, for example, the fifth year might be the opportunity to study the civilization and literature of non-western peoples. Others might take British history or a course in theater. The guideline does assume that no teacher of English will teach very long without discovering the need for more work in his own field. When the elementary teacher must cope with a variety of social, cultural, and regional dialects and when the secondary teacher must be able to select good literature for adolescents, courses that once seemed unimportant take on a new significance.

Any profession requires those who profess it to be engaged in the acquisition and evaluation of knowledge about it all of their lives. Therefore, the second guideline concludes with a recommendation that *The teacher of English at any level should consider growth in his profession as a continuing process.* No sensible man would consult a physician who had read no books or articles, heard no papers or reports from colleagues and research scientists in twenty years. Many English teachers, however, fail to keep up with their profession. College professors of English, in fact, buy surprisingly few books either within or outside their special fields.[28] Ironically, parents are often no more reluctant to change the English program in the schools than teachers: Shakespeare is, after all, Shakespeare. The lack of continuing education is a primary cause of such conservatism in the English teacher. Like the doctor who does not read medical journals or the stockbroker who does not follow the markets from day to day, the English teacher unaware of the startling changes now going on in English is woefully negligent. The person who becomes an English teacher, no matter how busy his life, will have to devote a certain number of hours a week to peruse the journals and books that will help him maintain and increase his professional competence. He must broaden his knowledge and understanding of the content and teaching of English through reading, observation, research of his own, formal course work, inservice study, workshops and institutes, and travel in the United States and abroad. One effective way to make this ambitious, lifelong commitment to a profession is through active membership in local, state, and national professional organizations. That teacher who complains that he hasn't time to read for his own pleasure or for his professional growth because of the hundreds of sophomore themes which are waiting to be graded might learn how to teach composition more effectively and even how to handle more easily the paperwork which confronts him if he would read a professional journal regularly. Engagement and involvement are key to the success of the teacher as well as of the student. No teacher of English wants his youngsters to leave his classroom hating English, vowing to avoid "literature" for the rest of his life; no teacher can complete his initial preparation for the classroom vowing that he, too, has had enough. While such personal qualities as a sense of humor are essential for the successful teacher of English, they cannot compensate for an ignorance about new directions in the teaching and learning of English which will grow more evident with each passing academic year. The self-discipline which leads a teacher to prepare his lessons and meet his classes cannot excuse his dedicated, but alas, outmoded defense of *I shall* or *different from*.

Most large school systems across the United States have initiated extensive inservice programs for teachers. Twenty-five hundred English teachers in Philadelphia, for example, met in September of 1967 to discuss the ETPS guidelines. Individual schools in smaller districts like Crystal Lake, Illinois, have also sponsored inservice courses on new curriculum materials in cooperation with nearby universities. By involving many members of the same department in a semester-long course or workshop, a high school can change its English program quickly because teachers learn together to understand new principles in linguistics and rhetoric, to select texts and other media, and to develop or adapt curriculum materials. More schools, particularly small secondary schools and elementary schools, need to sponsor informal workshops as well as courses in cooperation with college and university departments of English. The English professor will not only have much to contribute about English but much to learn about English programs in the schools. But perhaps the best place for the school teacher to take his inservice work is in his own school. If such on-the-spot inservice work is to become more prevalent in the 1970's, however, college English departments must not only be willing to design and staff new programs but also to design more effective ways of communicating with the schools. It is not enough for college departments of English to offer traditional, research-oriented graduate classes between nine and five on their own campuses. They must reassess not only what they teach for classroom teachers but even *when* they teach it if they are to meet the real needs of the schools. While professors reform their departments, individual classroom teachers must simultaneously make their needs known to the colleges and be committed to improving their skills and understandings.

Four years of summer institutes program in English funded by Title XI of the National Defense Education Act have shown that departments of English in colleges can work closely and effectively for and with teachers, but the institutes also frequently revealed not only enthusiasm but also woeful ignorance on the part of college departments. While the institute experiences of approximately 18,000 elementary and secondary teachers in some 440 NDEA English Institutes have been eminently worthwhile, they have demonstrated that only by trial and error can many college departments learn to develop or adapt graduate level courses to meet the needs of experienced teachers who face students every day of the school year. When a college like George Peabody in Nashville has an institute director like Lalla Walker, it can expect both a successful summer program and far-reaching effects on the surrounding region. If, on the other hand, a department does not staff its institutes with its best faculty members, if it does not reward those who engage in inservice work with teachers, if it uses institutes only to build or begin traditional graduate programs, if its administrative officers and senior professors do not visit or take part in the institute program, if the institute is seen only as a way of paying summer salaries, if programs are proposed without consultation with school teachers, if the department which has had one proposal for an institute rejected does not reconsider its program and apply again, then the English department is paying mere lip service to those inservice programs which are essential to any effective teacher preparation program.

School officials and classroom teachers have an opportunity to educate college faculty as well as learn from them. College faculty members who supervise practice teachers ordinarily come to the schools to observe student teachers (but seldom to teach elementary and secondary students themselves); those who have won distinction in their fields or engaged in appropriate research projects come to the schools to lecture, to consult, and to sip coffee with a busy faculty. But classroom teachers seldom invite college teachers of English to talk with their classes; to conduct special workshops; to consult about textbooks and paperbacks, new grammars, research in the teaching of composition, and current dialect studies. A far-reaching dialogue among professional English teachers at all levels has already begun; it must continue if college departments are to understand the needs of the classroom teacher and if classroom teachers are to participate actively in planning courses and sequences for teachers of English. Those who teach English at the college level to prospective teachers have seldom been in an elementary or junior high school, much less a middle school, either as observers or as demonstration teachers. Traditionalists who insist that the college professor of English is engaged in research into the subject matter of English and not its teaching, however important that may be, fail to realize that the great majority of college professors of English in the United States are not, in fact, engaged in research, that their preparation for teaching has been minimal if it has existed at all, and that they need experience with the schools as much to understand the students who later flock into their own classes as to enable them to present language and literature in ways which are intellectually and emotionally satisfying and yet relevant to the realities of the American schoolroom. The college professor has a responsibility to help to improve teacher preparation programs. Even a distinguished graduate professor should be willing to arrange to offer a class in a school rather than on his own campus if the school district can demonstrate its genuine interest in the subject matter of that course. Some graduate work, of course, can only be undertaken in research libraries, but that limitation cannot allow major departments to avoid their great responsibility to the total educational system.

Another objection to greater participation in the activities of the schools is that overcrowded colleges, like the schools themselves, can never find sufficient staff to engage in articulation programs. But this is not a satisfactory excuse for any chairman's failure to allocate part of his department's resources— no matter how limited—to the continuing education of teachers of English.

The Education Professions Development Act, which replaces the institute program of NDEA in 1969, will encourage school districts and colleges—both junior colleges and four-year institutions—to develop cooperative programs. The planning for such program has already begun through regional Triple-T Conferences for "Teachers of Trainers of Teachers." State supervisors, curriculum coordinators, college professors of English, and classroom teachers have attempted to define the areas in which each can help the other strengthen the school and college English program. The individual classroom teacher or professor can participate in such planning as part of his own continuing education. Although the schoolteacher sometimes feels that he cannot communicate with the college professor, each can and must contribute to the other's understanding of the teaching and learning of English if school programs are to be strong and not merely faddish, if students who go on to college are to be well prepared in English, if the English curriculum is to come under continuous and healthy reappraisal and reexamination. The development of the guidelines demonstrated that teachers of English at all levels could work together; the guidelines should now stimulate continuing discussion of the English curriculum, the new directions in English, the special, urgent problems of urban schools and of the disadvantaged throughout the United

States, and the pre- and inservice education of teachers of English for classrooms at every level.

How Much Content?

The third guideline, which is devoted to literature, begins with a general statement: *The teacher of English at any level should have an understanding and appreciation of a wide body of literature.* Five sections of the guideline investigate the teacher's personal interest in and response to literature, his systematic study of literature, his acquisition of critical and scholarly tools, his knowledge of literary works appropriate for the levels at which he teaches, and his study and practice of the strategies of teaching literature to students who have a wide variety of individual and group characteristics.

The teacher of English should first have a strong commitment to literature; to reading for his own enjoyment, for insight into himself and the world around him, and for the understanding and appreciation of the way in which writers order experience. Finding pleasure in literature and gaining knowledge from it are, of course, marks of any cultivated human being. The business executive, the physician, the scientist read for pleasure and for information. The English teacher, however, who will be formally engaged with literature throughout his professional life, has a special obligation—and a most pleasant one—to be committed to books. He must be able to share his genuine enthusiasm for books with his students, his colleagues, and with his family and friends, not necessarily by discussing what he reads but by sharing books he finds excellent and by encouraging the habit of reading in ways ranging from the quiet example of a love of books to the enthusiastic forcing of a favorite paperback on the teacher in the next classroom. One cannot, in fact, imagine a truly successful teacher of English or of the language arts who is not a book buyer and an omnivorous reader.

Although a personal commitment to literature is essential for the English teacher, he must also pursue it through systematic study. Unless he knows a wide range of significant works of literature; unless he has studied such major literary genres as drama, poetry, fiction, and the essay; unless he is acquainted with some important writers and writings which extend his knowledge of literary history and convention and develop his critical skills; unless he has read representative works from literature other than English and American; unless he has examined in depth the works of some major author, and at least one literary period, not only has he failed to experience the richness and diversity which characterize his discipline—he does not even command his subject. No student—no teacher in a lifetime—can read all the literature of even one period, but every professional must learn how rich the resources of his field are, and must have tested his interest in his subject and increased his command of it by reading a wide body of literature thoughtfully.

The teacher needs to know how to approach books. To develop these skills and refine his responses he should have studied different ways of analyzing a work of literature, including some formal training in the theories of literary criticism and practice in the close reading of texts. He must be able to analyze and discuss language as it is used in various media, and literature as it is presented in radio, television, motion pictures, and theater. In addition, he must be able to talk about these media as artistic ends in themselves.

The teacher of English will probably never utilize all that he knows in his own classroom. He must select appropriate critical techniques and literary works; he must incorporate media other than books when appropriate. No English class is more boring than that in which a teacher slavishly repeats the works, the critical methods, and the manner of presentation used by his college professors. The teacher can also contribute to a fuller understanding of literature in his class through reading aloud and through classroom activities such as individual oral interpretation, choral reading, and dramatic activities.

The teacher cannot foster in his students any taste for literature if he does not know literary works which are appropriate for the interest and maturity level of the students whom he teaches. Courses in children's literature or literature for adolescents have frequently, and often justifiably, been derided by academicians, but properly conceived and properly taught they have a legitimate place in the preparation program. English departments can guarantee the excellence of such courses most easily by increasing their own involvement in the planning and staffing of them.

The English classroom will be a stimulating place if students, whatever their age, are allowed to read and talk with one another about experiences and literature meaningful to them. The teacher who insists on imposing a set book, particularly one chosen because it is "classic," on a class takes the risk of stunting the linguistic and imaginative growth of his students. The study of *Silas Marner*, although it is still the most widely taught novel in the secondary school, is not finally the mark of an educated man.

The teacher must find ways to make students want to read and discuss books. The motivation must be generated by the students' previous discoveries about literature, by the books which they have read and wanted to share and discuss with one another. Here the teacher (particularly the college teacher) might ask: But what about the great books, what about learning the literary tradition, the tools of analysis? The answer is clear. If students find that the English classroom is filled only with artifacts, with shards and fossils, they will quickly lose their desire to read and talk, and their ability to respond to literature will be blunted.

The fourth guideline turns the reader's attention to language and composition: *The teacher of English at any level should have skill in listening, speaking, reading, and writing, and an understanding of the nature of language and of rhetoric.* Again the initial emphasis is on the teacher's personal skills. Not only should he be prepared in the technical and expository aspects of composition, but he should also have explored the creative and liberating functions of speaking and writing and the relations between such creativity and such other forms of expression as painting and pantomime. In emphasizing creative linguistic exploration, the guideline reflects the influence of the Dartmouth Conference most strongly.

Even though the guideline continues with recommendations for a "well-balanced descriptive and historical knowledge of the English language" and for a "functional understanding of the nature and substance of rhetoric," it carefully avoids emphasizing the acquisition of knowledge at the expense of imaginative and creative growth. How much and what the classroom teacher should know about language has worried and frustrated teachers of English since the "linguistics explosion" first exposed the deficiencies of school grammars. In order to use the textbooks now in the schools wisely and cautiously and to make intelligent choices of future texts and other teaching aids, the English teacher should have some understanding of phonology, morphology, and syntax; of the sources and development of the English vocabulary; of semantics; and of social, regional, and functional varieties of English usage. He should be acquainted, too, with methods of preparation and uses of dictionaries and grammars. He will need to become well grounded in one grammatical system—whether traditional, structural, transformational-generative, sectoral, tagmemic, or stratificational—and be acquainted with at least one other system. He must also apply what he has learned about the basic principles of language learning to the problems which his students face as they learn to speak, listen, read, and write to a variety of audiences. To his knowledge about language learning and language systems he should add some acquaintance with principles of classical rhetoric and their relationships to modern rhetoric. What he has discovered about rhetoric and the nature of the writing process will inevitably help him improve his own speaking, writing, and teaching.

No teacher on earth could master all these skills and accumulate all this knowledge in an undergraduate teacher preparation program. A well-balanced introduction to descriptive and historical linguistics and to rhetoric will, however, help him to teach students more effectively and will suggest the direction of his own future study. What teacher has not wished in a class on a given day that he knew more about dialectology or grammars or rhetorical principles so that he might answer a youngster's question, keep a lively discussion going, or help an individual child to use language more skillfully? The social as well as educational importance of coherent, soundly based language programs in the schools means that the American public school system cannot endure for long the English or language arts teacher who is not learning more each year about the ways in which human beings express themselves and communicate with one another. Today's schools particularly cannot support teachers who have inflated notions about the value of "correct usage," who inhibit a child's natural curiosity about language by enforcing rules and usages which at best characterize one dialect within American English and at worst are mere marks of snobbism, who confuse the teaching of writing with the teaching of usage. It is especially important that the teacher continue to study about language so that he may understand the characteristics of the dialects spoken by his students and know how to help them master a second standard dialect without losing pride in the dialect spoken in their homes and neighborhoods, so that he can motivate youngsters to express themselves orally and in writing. Far too many teachers of English, by emphasizing the mechanics or incidentals of a piece of student writing instead of its content and voice, seriously inhibit the linguistic growth of the child. For students to discard old notions and to learn to cope with new ones requires more of the teacher than a new set of textbooks; the attitudes toward language which condition the classroom come from the teacher's knowledge and experience. That knowledge must be accurate, up-to-date, the very best that is available to the teacher. And in the midst of a flood of research and publication about linguistics, the English teacher each year has access to more and more information about the ways in which people speak and write.

It is no exaggeration to say that linguistic naïveté on the part of the teacher of English in the urban school contributes to rioting in the streets and a hostility between community and school which the United States cannot afford in the next decade. Teachers must begin by dispossessing themselves of linguistic myths: Southerners have lazy speech habits; Boston English is "purer" than Bronx English; "ain't" is a mark of linguistic inferiority. The English teacher must admit that a student's ability to spell or punctuate, to write or recognize a compound-complex sentence or a 200-word paragraph which has unity and coherence is less important than his learning to speak openly and honestly, to listen well, to read many kinds of books and magazines and newspapers, and to write what he believes and thinks and feels. He should emphasize in his classroom that real skill in communication comes when a pupil has learned to find the proper voice, the best tone for a particular audience, and when he has something to say and is deeply committed to saying it.

Certainly the English teacher must have studied linguistics and rhetoric. If his knowledge can help students to develop a healthy curiosity about their language and skill in listening to others and in communicating effectively—even if not necessarily correctly—with others; if he makes them believe that speaking and writing can be effective ways of sharing experiences and of learning about oneself, the English teacher will be teaching language and composition well. If he fills classroom time teaching an elaborate grammatical system or principles of rhetoric *per se*, if he rules that a given number of misspelled words or sentence fragments will fail a paper automatically, no matter what the paper says, no matter how colorfully or effectively the writer says it, then the English teacher is doing a great disservice to his students by reinforcing the old belief that school is a sterile place which must be endured, a world of chalk dust and rules, a world divorced from the real concerns of students and of teachers.

But why should every teacher of English be asked to be well grounded in one grammatical system and to be acquainted with at least one other system? The guideline neither specifies which grammar the teacher ought to learn nor what place grammar has in the English classroom. When Paul Goodman suggests that professional teachers may have "to get rid of the educational establishment" in order to escape from teaching "subjects and answers" and begin watching "what the child is reaching for" and helping him to reach, he partially explains the place of grammar in the education of the teacher and of the student.[29] A grammar is valuable not because it prescribes the use of the language, corrects errors, or marks the educated man, but because it is a tool which describes how people speak and how our language operates. Some grammars approach one part of this task more effectively than others, but no system in existence today is complete. The teacher needs the intellectual base of one grammatical system, even if it is incomplete. Whatever he studies, however, should be as valid as current research permits. How much formal grammar he should introduce to youngsters and in which grades are topics currently under discussion. He should, of course, not spend valuable class time teaching school grammar, a watered-down traditional grammar both incomplete and highly prescriptive. He must not waste classroom time enforcing arbitrary standards of usage sometimes presented in textbooks as "grammatical rules." He should never teach a grammatical system at the expense of the child's interest in language. In the later elementary grades and in secondary school the teacher may well introduce some grammar because classroom activities and discussion will suggest that students want to know how to talk in increasingly sophisticated terms about the language they speak and write. While the transformational-generative grammar popularized by Noam Chomsky in the late 1950's and brought to the schools in the 1960's in the textbooks of Paul Roberts and others would seem the most valuable system for any teacher preparing to teach the textbooks of the 1970's, it has not replaced the sound traditional grammar best described by Otto Jespersen or the structural grammar which Charles Fries and others introduced into the schools. The teacher needs some acquaintance with a second grammatical system so that he can illustrate for students the various kinds of problems raised in any description of English.

Teaching the Student

The fifth guideline considers the learner and the learning situation: *The teacher of English at any level should have an understanding of the relationship of child and adolescent development to the teaching of English.* Not only should he have studied human behavior, with emphasis upon the age level at which he plans to teach (if he knows that level while he is still in school), but he should explore research on child and adolescent development for its possible implications for the curriculum in English. And he must have studied specifically the language development of children and adolescents, that is, their growth in the ability to distinguish among several varieties of usage. The teacher's focus in these studies will be upon the student as a human being to be understood and listened to as well as directed in the class-room. Because the teacher must constantly evaluate the perfor-mance of his students and the effectiveness of his own teaching, both subjectively and by diagnosing and measuring student per-formance, he should also understand the techniques, possibilities, and the limitations of testing and of grouping students by in-terest, aptitude, achievement, and task. Because research in some of these areas has only begun to produce significant reports, the guideline is particularly cautious. It can only recommend that the teacher "*be aware* of the *growing* knowledge about the re-lationships between language development and personal develop-ment" and "of the *growing knowledge* about the specific re-lationships between control of spoken language (sentence patterns, vocabulary, dialect) and success in reading." The importance of continuing education is again immediately apparent.

The obligation to become informed about human behavior is equally great for the college teacher. Charles Muscatine attacks the university's terrible "neglect of what we know about human growth and human development." "I do not feel," he writes, "that any university can survive much longer unless it begins to take account of what a young student is in terms of his growth and development and begins to make realistic allowance for those facts and for the fact that young people are different from each other." [30] Recent events at Columbia University and on dozens of other college and university campuses emphasize the importance of better understanding of student needs and interests by faculty and administration.

The emphasis in the guideline on the teacher's learning about the limitations of testing and of grouping as well as the tech-niques and possibilities reflects directly the concerns of the Dartmouth Seminar. Although those who met at Dartmouth could not agree on many aspects of English teaching, they unanimously stressed the importance of overcoming the "re-strictiveness of rigid patterns of 'grouping' or streaming which limit the linguistic environment in which boys and girls learn English and which tend to inhibit language development" and of negating "the limiting, often stultifying, impact of examination patterns." To discover what effects tests and examinations do have on the teaching and learning of English, the MLA, NCTE, and NATE have proposed a study to consider the impact of internal and external examinations on the student, the teacher, the school, and the community. If visits to selected schools in Canada, England, and the United States do support the suspicions of Dartmouth, they will have far-reaching effects on current American school practices.

In his *Search for Ability* (1963) and in articles in the *College Board Review* in 1967, sociologist David A. Goslin has perceptively discussed the controversies surrounding the widespread use of standardized tests in the United States. Although observing that "it would appear that the major growth of educational testing programs is over," [31] he has acknowledged the continuing difficulty of determining how much reliance is placed on test scores, either in decisions that are made about pupils (selection or allocation) or in determining what advice to give to pupils (counseling). Goslin's discussion of the effects of testing presents research which supports the hypothesis that a child "who does well on a test and, *as a consequence of his performance,* is placed in an advanced class or receives special attention from his teachers, or who is admitted to a good university, is more likely to do well in the future than the child who initially got a lower score on the test." [32] The position of the Dartmouth participants also gains support from Goslin's studies: "Research indicates that . . . differentiation within schools may have a negative effect on the performance levels of low-ability pupils. In addition, it is clear that ability grouping impedes the process of acculturation of members of culturally deprived groups, who tend to end up together in the low-ability groups" (p. 34). His considered recommendation is "that we must begin thinking about tests in much broader perspective; one that considers their social effects as well as one that merely considers their validity and reliability" (p. 37).

Testing and grouping are also problems of real consequence for the college English department. I suspect that few college professors know much about the techniques of testing and measurement. The examination which the individual college faculty member prepares for his literature or composition course may often be a classic example of bad testing practices. The college teacher, in fact, is unlikely to have read any studies dealing with the possibilities and limitations of multiple choice, short answer, or essay tests. He chooses arbitrarily what he *thinks* will be appropriate for his students. In grouping students for freshman English courses, many departments continue to depend upon testing instruments which measure only the student's grasp of school grammar and of standard usage. The educational, economic, professional, and social effects of the comprehensive examinations for the doctorate force university departments to review their examination practices even more carefully. Noting that "It is preposterous to try to grade a lecture course," Charles Muscatine urges the university community "to reject much of the prison routine of examining and grading every week and every month and every semester" (p. 21). The controversies about testing and the serious challenges to traditional testing methods in the school and in the college make it essential for the English teacher to know enough about testing and measurement to examine his own testing practices and those current in his department.

The final guideline turns attention to the development of the teacher's professional skills: *The teacher of English at any level should have studied methods of teaching English and have had supervised teaching.* The elementary teacher should have had supervised teaching or an internship which included the language arts under supervisors prepared in this area, should be able to relate the language arts to other parts of the school curriculum, and should be aware of recent developments in the teaching of English. The secondary school teacher should have been guided by someone who has recently taught English successfully at that level and who is aware of recent developments in the teaching of English. This recommendation again envisions an educational community in which both professor and classroom teacher move freely between the school and the college campus. The specialist in English or in English Education who supervises student teaching regularly has the opportunity to take over classes and to demonstrate lessons in the elementary and secondary school classroom and to discuss with teachers the methods and materials necessary to teach English well on their home grounds. The classroom teacher continues, at the same time, to use the resources of the university in his program of continuing education. Dean Roald F. Campbell of the Graduate School of Education at the University of Chicago has also urged this "joining of professors in the disciplines with teachers in the schools" in an essay predicting that "scholars in the basic disciplines will be required to give help in the development of school subjects" in tomorrow's schools at the same time that teachers acquire "greater specialization" through inservice programs which "become much more of the regular work expectation of most teachers." [32]

The teacher of English should also have practiced a range of teaching techniques and learned to analyze units of instruction, prepare lessons and materials, and understand and evaluate the development and design of courses of study. Again reflecting the concerns of Dartmouth, the guideline specifies that the candidate for teaching should study and practice ways to foster creativity in the speaking and writing of his students and learn to select, adapt, and develop activities and materials appropriate to different age groups distinguished by maturity, culture, ability, and achievement, and to individual students.

The guideline also asks the prospective teacher of English to create, find, evaluate, and use "significant instructional materials from various media." Despite the idle fears expressed by some educators and the extravagant claims made by some manufacturers, the printed page will not disappear from the English classroom in the 1970's any more than the book will cease to be an important part of the life of the American intellectual. The teacher of English—or any other subject—who once boasted that he never watched television and had no intention of buying a set now finds that he must make television and other new media a regular part of his intellectual and cultural life. As Edmund J. Farrell notes, "Anyone who now ignores a medium found in over fifty million households within the nation and regularly viewed by over 90 percent of its population can not be overly concerned with the culture in which he lives or the people with whom he must communicate." [33] Farrell goes so far as to suggest that the teacher who ignores television "abjures a professional if not ethical responsibility to help students develop sound taste for all artistic media." Teachers of English have been particularly suspicious of new media within the classroom. Until very recently, as William G. Harley, President of the National Association of Educational Broadcasters, points out, they were correct in assuming that the utilization of technology in education "resulted in a subtraction of time from the teacher instead of giving him time to pursue the neglected human relationships of education." [34] If technology is to become "capable of effecting comprehensive change" in the classroom, however, teachers of English must participate in a reexamination of the "role of the teacher, the role of the classroom, the nature of the learning process itself" in the light of new technology. Even as profound changes are being discussed, however, the teacher of English must be able to utilize the equipment and facilities already available to him. Farrell, arguing convincingly that "newer media be given a legitimate share of classroom time," observes, "In no class in English should television, for example, be totally ignored, nor should it necessarily be given status inferior to that of print." His final clause strikes terror into the hearts of conservative English teachers who are already upset by the new grammars, experimental curriculums, and growing professional demands on the classroom teacher. For the well-prepared teacher in the schools or colleges, however, the growing possibilities of media promise a more challenging English classroom in the next decade.

Finally, the sixth guideline asks the prospective teacher to consider the problems of censorship in American education. If he has thought about and discussed the kinds of situations which can arise in class through the introduction of certain topics and books, he will be better prepared to handle situations which do arise. The teacher who tries to make his classroom relevant to the larger world in which youngsters live may need to expose students to ideas alien to their own cultural backgrounds. He must be particularly wary of pressure groups within the community which seek to ban books because they are "dirty" or "un-American" or "too fantastic" for young people. As NCTE studies have demonstrated, almost every major piece of literature by an American author has been banned from one classroom or another in company with the poems, plays, novels, and essays of such distinguished British writers as Geoffrey Chaucer, William Shakespeare, and Jonathan Swift. There are many secondary school libraries in the United States which contain more books about William Faulkner, for example, than copies of his novels. *The Adventures of Huckleberry Finn,* a superb plea for tolerance and brotherhood, has been ignorantly attacked because Mark Twain uses the word "nigger." Accounts of the condemnation of the *Girl Scout Handbook* as "un-American" and of the ultra-conservatism of the Daughters of the American Revolution which Jack Nelson and Gene Roberts, Jr. relate in *The Censors and the Schools* (1963) would be amusing if they did not bear witness to the authors' conclusion that "In some parts of the United States it is worth a teacher's job to put modern novels such as J. D. Salinger's *The Catcher in the Rye* or George Orwell's *1984* on a classroom reading list." [35] It is appalling to know that such cases of censorship are increasing each year in the schools of the United States.

The prospective teacher needs to be aware that such groups as the American Library Association, the American Civil Liberties Union, and the NCTE are prepared to provide him with advice and counsel in cases of censorship. The NCTE has published, for example, an important pamphlet entitled *The Students' Right to Read* which helps the teacher interpret his role in the classroom to an interested parent.[36] The pamphlet discusses the dangers of censorship clearly and openly:

> Many well-meaning persons wish to restrict school reading to books that do not mention unsavory aspects of our society. They argue that children must not be exposed to books in which people drink or swear or do many of the things commonly featured in daily newspapers, on television, or in motion pictures. No more than the people who condemn these books are teachers interested in promoting drinking and swearing. What the teacher sees as his responsibility, however, is to lead his students to understand all aspects of their culture and society—the good and the bad. This he can best do by cultivating

in his students an appreciation for the wise and enduring thoughts of great writers. This he cannot do if major literary documents interpreting our culture are cut off from his students.

The NCTE recognizes, however, as the teacher must, that the parent has a right to inquire about the texts which his children are using in the English classroom. Often censorship arises when there has been a breakdown in communication between teacher or school administrator and parent or community. To assist the parent with a legitimate complaint, the NCTE has provided a "Citizen's Request for Reconsideration of a Book," which outlines, step by step, the way to prepare a forceful case for a reconsideration. The parent who objects can indicate what he objects to, whether he finds the entire book objectionable or only parts, and for what age level he thinks it appropriate. The teacher must know how to choose books responsibly and defend his choices.

The guidelines developed by the English Teacher Preparation Study clearly have much to say about the teaching of English at all levels of education as well as about the preparation of teachers of English for the elementary and secondary schools. The six major guidelines and the dozens of supplementary recommendations are a call for commitment to departments of English and to individual English teachers. Although visionary in some respects, the guidelines offer practical direction to any of the nearly 1100 college departments of English working to strengthen teacher preparation programs at either the undergraduate or graduate level. For the teacher of English now in the schools the recommendations outline a lifetime program of continuing education. For the college professor of English they offer a challenge to participate in the revitalization of the most important subject in the American curriculum.

The English Teacher in the Two-Year College

Addressing a national conference on the teaching of English in the junior college sponsored by the NCTE and the Conference on College Composition and Communication at Arizona State University in 1965, Albert H. Kitzhaber identified two related problems of growing importance to the English profession: "how to improve the competence, how to update and increase the knowledge of the people already teaching English in two-year colleges" and "how to recruit more teachers who are both skilled and well grounded in their subjects." [37] A large part of the problem in the English curriculum in the junior and community college could be attributed, H. K. Newburn noted, to "the inadequate—or more properly stated—the nonexistent program for the preparation of junior college teachers. The sooner we recognize the uniqueness of the junior college and begin to prepare teachers specifically for work in this institution, the more likely we are to resolve the problem satisfactorily." [38] The Tempe Conference, as it came to be called, "recommended as a responsibility of the colleges and universities a detailed five-year program of English preparation, which would include emphasis on studying the particular nature of teaching English in the junior college." Most current graduate programs in English, as Roger Garrison points out in *Junior College Faculty: Issues and Problems,* are "inappropriate for the needs" of teachers of English in the two-year colleges. "There is a strong desire, strongly expressed," Garrison adds, "for more graduate offerings designed to assist teachers with the problems of freshman and sophomore instruction. . . . Again and again, *sharply,* was the desire expressed to take a new, and possibly unorthodox look, at the materials and teaching methods in freshman and sophomore years. . . ." As a result of his conversations with hundreds of junior college faculty members, Garrison also envisioned a program which included a "minimum of ten courses (or equivalent) in the subject discipline *at the graduate level,*" half of which would be "to the greatest degree possible, *interdisciplinary* in content and in instruction." [39]

While Kitzhaber looked forward to the establishment of a "new terminal teaching degree" for the junior college teacher of English, Garrison saw only the need for a "certificate of internship experience and completion of professional seminar" in addition to the ordinary master of arts degree. Before the issues of graduate requirements and advanced degrees for junior college teachers can be resolved, however, the profession must study more carefully the part which the junior and community college plays in higher education and the responsibilities which face the teacher of English in a two-year college. In the community college especially, the English teacher instructs students with an extremely wide range of abilities. He must create a humane, intellectual climate in which each of these students can discover his potential. He must also help to make the college a vital force in the life of the community. To help prepare college teachers of English to succeed in these tasks and to assist those teachers already working on more than 900 two-year college campuses, the NCTE, MLA, and AAJC have followed Garrison's directive to undertake the development of "Guidelines for graduate work appropriate to the training of teachers" for these colleges. The study, to be completed in 1969, is also helping to establish more regular conversations between professors of English and their colleagues in the junior colleges, to encourage the institution of graduate programs specially designed for two-year college teachers, and to resolve the whole issue of the place of the intermediate degree in American higher education. If these guidelines are as influential as those which emerged from the English Teacher Preparation Study and from the study of the Ph.D. in English and American literature, it will be in no small part because of the important preliminary work done by Samuel Weingarten and Frederick Kroeger in *English in the Two Year College*.[40] Their influential report not only provided the basic information about the teaching of English in junior and community colleges which directed the discussion at Tempe, but helped to stimulate the establishment of the six successful regional conferences on English in the two-year college organized by the NCTE and the CCCC in 1966.

The proper course of teacher preparation in English for the junior and community college teacher has not yet been determined. Only a few institutions such as the University of Tennessee and the University of Iowa now offer graduate programs broadly enough conceived to train both the research scholar and the college teacher. The pressures on graduate schools to supply well-trained college English teachers will continue to grow throughout the next decade. The wide range of intellectual ability and interest which characterizes the junior college student population suggests, in addition, that these teachers must be qualified to instruct not only the highly motivated college bound or transfer student but the vocationally oriented student and the adult who wishes to use his leisure time to continue his education. The new teacher preparation programs which are developed in the graduate schools will inevitably combine substantive work in English with study in psychology, sociology, and urban affairs. Internships or supervised practice teaching on the junior college campus and an exchange of faculty between the graduate department and the two-year college department will also promote effective teaching at all levels of higher education. Until guidelines which emphasize college teaching have been developed and widely implemented in graduate departments of English, however, the junior college itself will have to maintain extensive inservice programs to acquaint teachers with the special problems and special rewards of teaching English in the two-year college.

The college and university teacher himself will have much to learn from those teaching and developing curriculum in junior colleges. At present, many junior colleges base their introductory courses in composition and literature for transfer students on the work required by the senior colleges. The direction of freshman English programs, the nature of introductory literature courses, and the sequence of courses taken by the transfer students continuing on to the senior college will, however, be more and more determined by the faculties of the junior and community colleges. By the middle of the 1970's, few senior college departments—and certainly not those located in the state universities—will be able to refuse to transfer credits in English earned by students in the two-year colleges. The director of freshman English in the large university department may, in fact, find the nature of his job changing radically. Instead of supervising a large freshman English staff and planning courses in English composition and literature on his own campus, he will probably become the principal liaison officer between the junior college and the university department, the person responsible for the orderly transfer of student credits and the closest kind of cooperation with the junior college faculty on the development of curriculum. What the junior college department chooses to teach will determine for many American colleges and universities the quality of the preparation of the potential English major. Articulation, then, becomes of vital importance to the college teacher, whether he teaches in the two-year or four-year institution.

The Place of English Education

Better teacher preparation programs, greater involvement with schools and two-year colleges, and new emphasis on excellence in teaching must lead college English departments to examine the role of the specialist in English Education. While only a few universities—New York University and Florida State University, for example—have well-established, separate departments of English Education, many large departments of English have made appointments to their own faculties or given joint appointments with Education to professors whose special interest is English Education. Although more departments wish to make similar appointments each year from the small pool of available specialists, the college teaching community has only begun to give proper recognition to the college teacher who is professionally interested in teaching methods and materials, curriculum development, the supervision of student teachers, and articulation with the schools. If departments wish to improve their programs for the preparation of English teachers for the schools, they will have to offer to the specialist in English Education greater opportunities for advancement and a voice in setting departmental policies. If the graduate departments wish to implement the recommendation of the Allen report on the Ph.D. calling for supervised practice teaching, they will need to draw upon the special skills of the specialist in English Education. Ironically enough, the faculty member who is perhaps most clearly fulfilling the department's responsibility to influence American public education often suffers from the condescension of his peers. He is accepted reluctantly, promoted slowly, and accused of neglecting the erudite special field in which he did his advanced work in English. His research is considered "unimportant" or "second-rate" by other members of the department. Even though he is often expected to have met all of the standard requirements for the Ph.D. in English, he must take additional work to learn enough about curriculum building, teaching techniques, statistics, and supervision to do justice to the students whom he will serve. Only a few universities such as Florida State, Minnesota, Nebraska, and Stanford have established graduate programs in English Education which regularly produce distinguished professors of English education.

Through the efforts of the Conference on English Education, a section of the NCTE, the field of English Education is gaining strength in departments of English and new doctoral programs to prepare specialists are currently being planned in several institutions. In 1967 the CEE authorized Dwight Burton of Florida State to poll one hundred leading specialists about their own educational backgrounds, their recommendations for establishing graduate programs in English Education, and their ideas of the functions of specialists in English Education in the college department of English. A conference of professors of English and of Education, graduate deans and deans of education, and school teachers and administrators held in May 1968 led to specific recommendations which will assist any departments wishing to make full use of the professor of English Education or to establish graduate programs in English Education leading to the master's degree or the doctorate. The recommendations are designed not only to outline the kind of preparation which should be required of the English Education specialist and his role in both departments, but to help establish a climate in which joint appointments have the enthusiastic approval of both departments, as at Stanford or Northwestern, for example, and in which promotion, salary increments, and recognition by colleagues and by the administration are as available to the man in English Education as to the specialist in linguistics, in Shakespeare, or in Milton. Through the recommendations and conferences of the CEE, graduate departments have the opportunity to establish programs which will produce scholar-teachers qualified to work with prospective teachers for the schools, junior and community colleges, and colleges and universities and to generate curriculum revision in teacher preparation at all levels.

Institutions have an unusual opportunity to develop programs for the preparation and improvement of teachers through the Education Professions Development Act of 1967. The Act, which amends the Higher Education Act of 1965 and replaces Title XI of NDEA, provides funds not only to attract qualified persons to the field of education and to provide fellowships in higher education, but also to establish programs to train persons who are serving or preparing to serve as teachers, administrators, or educational specialists in institutions of higher education. Particularly in 1969 and 1970 funds will be available to cover the costs of courses of study, either for short terms or regular academic-year programs, and for fellowships. Although there have been limited funds available to assist students preparing for careers in college teaching through 1968, the thrust of federal support has been toward the reeducation of teachers, administrators, and supervisors for the schools, both through the NDEA institutes in English which began in 1965 and through such other programs as the Prospective and Experienced Teacher Fellowship Programs authorized by the Higher Education Act of 1965. In 1967–1968, for example, academic-year programs in English for teachers, administrators, and supervisors were held on six campuses. While Arizona State University conducted a program for teachers of the disadvantaged in grades seven through twelve in the southwestern United States, Florida State worked with twenty-five prospective supervisors in grades seven through twelve in Florida, and the University of Illinois at Urbana brought together twenty prospective secondary English department chairmen from across the United States. In the summer of 1968, eighty-five institutes, including six for college teachers of teachers, demonstrated the wide range of inservice programs available for American English teachers. EPDA will now extend many of these opportunities to the entire college teaching community.

Arthur Eastman gloomily predicted in 1967 that there was little hope "that the English classroom will escape much longer public damnation as the number one disaster area in the Anglo-American school and college," a note struck earlier by Daniel Bell in *The Reforming of General Education,* who found the teaching of English "so poor as to threaten the nation's entire educational system." [41] Even if the reform of teacher preparation programs in English cannot take place as quickly as the needs of the schools and of American society demand, there is hope that the studies which have been noted in this chapter will lead to rapid improvement in the quality of English teachers and to that improvement of English teaching which must inevitably follow.

chapter three

English, Education, and Change

Why Education Changes

Change in American education has accelerated since 1958. New patterns of school organization, newly felt community pressures, new media, and the new activism of teachers modify the structure of the neighborhood school more significantly each fall. Universal education to the age of twenty, student activism, and the success of the "commuter college" affect the plans of every college and university in the United States. State and federal support for education at all levels, although unhappily curtailed by the pressures of war and politics, encourage experimental classrooms, schools, and educational parks. So many projects and studies have contributed to change at the local, state, and national levels in the 1960's that no educator could begin to evaluate them all. While major projects supported by the Office of Education and the Office of Economic Opportunity receive the attention of both press and public, hundreds of worthwhile local programs have gone relatively unnoticed. Such crucial issues as equal educational opportunities for disadvantaged youngsters and the bargaining rights of teachers necessarily obscure dozens of other very real issues about the future of American education.

Not every English teacher can or should be expected to become a curriculum specialist, a professional leader, a lobbyist for education in a state legislature or in Congress, or the master of every piece of gadgetry which appears on the market. He will find it impossible, in fact, even to study the myriad reports about education which flow across his desk each week. Yet he must learn about experiments with school organization and curriculum, media, information retrieval systems, and controversial issues in education which can affect his classroom and his teaching. This chapter, therefore, tries to identify a number of notable experiments and to discuss a series of major issues in education which will influence the teaching and learning of English in school and college in the next decade.

The education of the disadvantaged is probably the major educational issue in the United States today.

As parents in ghetto areas demand a voice in the development of curriculum and in the administration of schools, as the union drives to improve working conditions in schools in deprived areas, as city governments initiate studies and reports on educational opportunities for the disadvantaged, and as the federal government pours billions of dollars into experimental programs, the English teacher is forced to consider the quality of his preparation, his autonomy in the classroom, the relevance of what he teaches, and his involvement with the community. The college professor, too, must accept new responsibilities for establishing the English program in these schools.

Again, decisions by the states to build statewide junior college systems force the college English teacher to ask important questions: How should junior college teachers be trained? What kinds of articulation will insure that the transfer student adjusts to the English program in a four-year college or university? How will the traditional freshman English course change in the 1970's as the junior college provides the instruction for three-quarters of all students entering college? Graduate professors of English have an obligation to explore the possibilities of internships for graduate students in the junior and community colleges, to plan inservice programs for two-year college teachers, and to examine carefully such mundane matters as the effects of current selective service regulations on graduate study in English. Union representation and collective bargaining in colleges and schools raise questions about the traditional relationship between a teacher and his administration which cannot be ignored by any teacher of English.

Three factors have been particularly responsible for changes in the American school in the past decade: a new vision of the teacher as a professional person, the growth of school populations, and a commitment to excellence. Although changes have been less dramatic in small schools like Paxton High School in Paxton, Illinois, than in major secondary schools like New Trier and Nova, change is apparent everywhere. Educational reform has become, in fact, an influence so pervasive in American society that no city or town, no college community or ghetto has remained untouched.

As the teacher in the schools works to obtain better teaching conditions, to increase his salary, and to raise his status in society, he profoundly affects the school and the community. Through collective bargaining, he exerts a new power in the administrative structure of the school and school district. He asks for a greater say in curriculum planning, inservice programs, and school administration as well as more manageable class sizes and teaching loads. He asks to be relieved of onerous extra duties which interfere with his professional growth: lunchroom supervision, hall guard duty, excessive paper work and record keeping, and the sponsorship of a variety of student activities. In far too many secondary schools the English teacher can still expect to be assigned to be moderator of the debate club, director of the school plays, and adviser to the newspaper and yearbook without being given either adequate extra compensation or a reduced teaching load. Ironically, effective collective bargaining can also interfere with the teacher's professional responsibility to work with students outside of class time. The administration which must pay overtime to any teacher who stays beyond the last school bell does not readily encourage after-school conferences and tutorials.

To supplement and balance the gains which come to the public school teacher from effective union representation, he needs effective leadership from his professional associations. The NCTE, representing 135,000 teachers and subscribers, has frequently provided that leadership for teachers of English. Its policy statements on the workloads of teachers of English at various levels are striking examples. The Council has not only called for a maximum teaching load for secondary teachers of four classes with not more than twenty-five students in each class, but published an "Honor Roll of Schools Reducing Teaching Load in English" since 1962. Although James R. Squire reported as recently as 1966 that even 55.4% of the English teachers in his *Study of English Programs in Selected High Schools Which Consistently Educate Outstanding Students in English* were still meeting five classes each day and that only 21.0% met fewer than 100 pupils per day, the NCTE recommendations have helped to reduce the teaching load in hundreds of American high schools (pp. 69–70).

In November, 1967, the Board of Directors of the NCTE unanimously adopted a policy statement on *The Workload of the Elementary School Teacher* calling for self-contained elementary school classes "limited to 25 pupils." The five recommendations noted that in "patterns of organization other than the self-contained class, children may be grouped in larger or smaller units at different times," but warned that "teachers of English in such arrangements, however, should teach no more than 75 pupils per day, nor should the class exceed 25 pupils for one teacher."

The NCTE published its third policy statement, on *The Workload of a College English Teacher,* in *College English* in October, 1966. It recommended a "weekly teaching load of no more than nine hours" as the standard load for college teachers of English and warned that *"under no circumstances* should any English teacher's weekly load exceed 12 hours," a goal not yet reached in nearly a third of the colleges in the United States.[1] Thomas Wilcox, in a preliminary report on his findings in the National Survey of Undergraduate English Programs, noted that about "50% of departments have normal teaching loads of 12 hours." [2] In fifteen per cent of all departments, he reported, the teaching load is still ordinarily fifteen class hours per week or more. Only 0.7% of the institutions in his random sample could boast of an across-the-board teaching load of six hours or fewer. The fifteen-hour load is most common in the southeastern United States and least common in the North Atlantic. Those institutions with graduate programs in English do not have a significantly smaller teaching load than those without such programs. Wilcox discovered, further, that "81% of those replying to the questionnaire believe that the English department's teaching load compares favorably with those of all other departments," [3] a statistic which Dean William Buckler of New York University felt obligated to challenge in an address to the chairmen of college English departments in December 1967: "I am reasonably sure that this is not true; I am reasonably sure that the statistics upon which it is based—belief rather than knowledge—are unreliable; and I am positive that the publication of it as a fact will, unless corrected, undermine the value of the report." [4] Dean Buckler refuted Professor Wilcox's statistics on the basis of his own administrative experience and argued, "If true, it means that chairmen of the largest and strongest departments have accepted the average lot, despite the guidelines of their largest professional association. If false, it means that chairmen of the largest and strongest departments, in the face of the guidelines of their largest professional association, have abdicated administrative leadership" (p. 7). The NCTE guidelines have obviously sparked both research and lively discussion. Professor Wilcox's study will enable departments throughout the United States to compare their teaching loads with those of similar departments in other institutions and to judge the applicability of the NCTE recommendations for their own situations. Dean Buckler's incisive remarks should stimulate chairmen and their faculties to examine not only teaching loads but their responsibility for intellectual leadership in the college.

The *Vacancy Lists* of faculty positions available in colleges and universities throughout the United States and Canada published by the Association of Departments of English also inform the college teaching profession about current teaching loads, salaries, and faculty benefits. Working with the Modern Language Association, the ADE also operates the principal faculty exchange service for teachers of English in higher education. Each December during the annual meeting of the MLA, more than 500 chairmen interview nearly 2,000 candidates for faculty appointments for the next fall. It is to the advantage of both the chairman and the candidate to know as much as possible about the current range of academic salaries, the supply of and demand for various kinds of specialists, typical teaching loads, and the kinds of courses which faculty members at various ranks can be expected to teach. The services and statements of the professional associations, clearly in accord with the goals of the unions, the National Education Association, and the American Association of University Professors, represent the English profession's attempt to help the college teacher find the faculty appointment for which he is best suited and to establish professional standards within departments of English. Organized labor and the associations in English are not yet in competition for the loyalties of the teacher of English. As long as the associations continue to provide English teachers with thoughtful, responsible, practical leadership in professional matters, labor and the associations can work hand in hand to improve the professional status of the teacher of English and the effectiveness of the English classroom. The demise of the NEA as the voice of the classroom teacher and indications that the AAUP cannot continue to represent the college faculty in competition with the unions suggest how important it is for the discipline-oriented associations to take public stands and to concern themselves with professional issues. The college English community can choose to devote itself solely to scholarship, to ignore professional issues, to oppose unionization on the campus or it can develop an effective professional voice and provide intellectual leadership for the labor movement which will soon reach almost every American college.

As school populations grow, teachers, administrators, curriculum planners, and school board members must find ways to use existing facilities more effectively, to build new schools which reflect the best educational planning, and to develop curriculums suitable for students of greatly varying abilities. While many small schools still exist in the United States, the continuing flow of population to urban centers and the consolidation of school districts in states like Nebraska have led to a growing number of large schools which must offer a wide range of courses to able, average, and slow students. The baby boom, which flooded the elementary schools a few years after World War II, had begun to abate by 1967, but enrollment pressures on secondary schools and on the colleges continue to grow because more students are entering school, staying in school, and going on to college. In addition, adults, faced with increasing amounts of leisure time, turn to continuing education programs both as a source of entertainment and of enrichment. Many flock to literature and writing courses, not always for reasons which the teacher finds admirable.

Although some excellent small colleges such as Duchesne in Omaha have closed their doors because of dwindling enrollments and limited financial resources and many other small colleges have joined their resources in order to remain in existence, junior and community colleges have been appearing at the rate of better than one new college each week, a growth rate which will continue for the next decade. Once established, these two-year colleges increase their student populations at a truly fantastic rate. As he attempted to locate twenty-five new classrooms for the fall of 1968, the president of a community college in Rhode Island noted that his enrollment had jumped from 300 in 1965 to 1300 in 1966 and to 2500 in 1967. He could only guess what 1968 would bring. Those who have studied the junior college movement (by 1970 one hundred junior colleges will enroll nearly one million students in California alone) estimate that by the mid 1970's three-quarters of all the English that is taught in college will be taught in junior and community colleges and that three-quarters of the college English faculty will be in these colleges. As they grow, the junior colleges must plan new English programs appropriate for the different kinds of students who are now flocking to college. The universities, now strengthening their graduate programs and reexamining their undergraduate programs, can plan new curriculum patterns well only if they consult with their colleagues in two-year colleges and in the growing state colleges. When an institution like the State College of Pennsylvania at Indiana finds itself raised to the Indiana State University of Pennsylvania and is called upon to establish graduate programs which will help to meet the critical shortage of college faculty in English and in other disciplines, the established university departments and the professional associations as well as local junior and community colleges must offer generous amounts of help. More students and more programs are bringing new responsibilities and opportunities to departments of English at every level of education.

Excellence in the schools is achieved only as the public becomes more aware of the role of education in society. Even when taxpayers have defeated bond issues for new schools and better salaries and working conditions for teachers, they have been forced to engage in a dialogue with educators which awakens the community to the problems of the schools. When such awareness exists, a community can begin to move toward educational change. In Harlem parents have demanded the right to help select school administrators and to set goals for educational programs in the schools. In Brooklyn, parents have banded together to plan with school officials ways to reflect community needs more adequately in the schools. For ten years the United States has been striving for excellence in its schools. The teacher and scholar have worked to develop new curriculums. The administrator and legislator have sought and used funds to improve school plants and facilities. Parents have participated more and more in the discussion of school goals. So much attention to education can, of course, breed rash behavior and irresponsible innovation. Far more often, it builds better schools.

How Change Takes Place
Although the very magnitude of the educational establishment causes such major problems of the American schools as overcrowding, the need for better facilities, and the shortage of qualified teachers, it presents, at the same time, a continuous series of opportunities for curriculum change, sparked as much by the pressing needs of the school as by the desire to innovate. The teacher facing a large class of Spanish-speaking children in the grade schools of a ghetto in a major city must, for example, not only locate books designed to teach English to speakers of other languages but experiment with games and songs that will motivate youngsters to learn English. Furthermore, he must work closely with parents and community leaders to win support for school programs. He may, indeed, invite parents to attend and

participate in their children's classrooms and may offer special classes for the parent themselves. A system of education which directly touches the lives of nearly thirty percent of the total population of the United States and spends in excess of 52 billion dollars a year can be characterized as mastodonic, but even casual investigation will show that it also produces hundreds of excellent new school programs each year. In 125,803 schools and 2,337 colleges and universities in 1967, more than 57 million students encountered both exciting and insipid teachers, bold curriculum patterns and out-of-date textbooks, classrooms equipped with many media and rooms without sufficient seats for all the class. The national effort to bring excellence to this gigantic enterprise has led into the schools dozens of new textbook publishers, manufacturers of a hundred kinds of hardware from the Language Master to the overhead projector, and businessmen and fund-raising consultants. Industry and publishing have designed "mixed-media" packages, combining books, films, film strips, records, and slides, which can change the face of the English classroom. Commissioned by, tested in, sold to, and purchased for outstanding school systems, these packages demonstrate not only the interest in education which becomes more apparent in business every year but the significant contributions which business and industry can make to education.

With more than 11 million college graduates in the United States and with a growing trend toward specialization in every field, business, industry, and government, as well as the colleges and universities, find themselves establishing college-credit courses, inservice programs, even sabbaticals for the further education and intellectual stimulation of their employees. It is a rare executive who has not attended a workshop or seminar on a university campus during the past year. Working with universities, many businesses have set up programs which parallel established graduate work in business and in the sciences. The universities now find that they must frequently send both administrators and scholars to industrial giants like IBM to learn to use the sophisticated computers which are changing education. As education touches the lives of more and more Americans, the academy and the business sector have been brought closer and closer together. Many educators, especially in the humanities, fear the interchange between the academic community and the "Philistines." Without that free and regular interchange of services, ideas, and opinions, however, education will suffer as greatly as business and government.

John Goodlad has identified the major directions of the curriculum reform of the past decade in *The Changing School Curriculum* (1966). One characteristic of curriculum change since 1958, he notes, has been the "emphasis on updating and reorganizing those academic disciplines that are considered basic in the pre-collegiate curriculum." [5] Anyone who has examined the work of Project English would agree that the curriculum movement has been marked, in Goodlad's words, "by an updating of content, a reorganization of subject matter, and some fresh approaches to methodology in fields traditionally taught in the schools. It is not simply a return to the Three R's. Nor is it a rejection of John Dewey and progressive education." He notes that the "first wave of the current curriculum reform was initiated at the secondary school level and has refined some initial assumptions. The second wave . . . focuses on the elementary school and is more experimental in character; it questions the earlier assumptions, and in all probability will initiate a fresh round of curriculum revision for the high school." A third wave is only beginning to reach the colleges, which still seem relatively unaffected by the great school interest in linguistics, for example, and still too often consider the English major as a literature major. Goodlad also points out that "trainers of teachers are not learning enough about the new curriculum movement," an observation which John Maxwell reinforces in his advice to classroom teachers in the December 1967 *English Journal* [6] and one which could easily be applied to the majority of college English departments. Goodlad was worried, because "While . . . reform is closing a long-standing´gap between curriculum theory and school practice, it has not been able so far to influence the content and pedagogy in those colleges and universities that prepare tomorrow's teachers, educational leaders, and teachers of teachers. And until it does, it has no means for self-renewal." The programs and studies outlined in the first two chapters suggest how the English profession has approached these three goals, but they do not emphasize a crucial fourth wave of reform—the integration of education into the total fabric of American life. How can the field of English become more meaningful to a growing population interested in education and especially in the impact of education on American society? This fourth wave will require the teacher of English, working with the psychologist, the sociologist, the urban planner, and business and industry, to consider carefully the educational needs of adults as well as children and adolescents and to prepare to educate great masses of citizens outside the teaching profession, citizens who have no intention of entering teaching. The first chapter of this volume asks the English profession to examine the curriculum in the schools and colleges; the second calls for greatly improved teacher preparation programs in English at all levels; this third chapter is, most of all, a plea to English teachers to find ways to integrate education in English into the fabric of a complex, sophisticated, modern society.

Before the English teacher can become responsive to the needs of society at large, he must first understand the students in his own classes. Critics of the schools such as John Holt, Herbert Kohl, and James Herndon have noted the rigidity of the curriculum and administration of the schools and the failure of educators to give students real responsibility and self-respect. They have also pointed out the irrelevancy of much of the school curriculum for today's students and the oppressiveness of the testing and grouping patterns in almost every school. In one of the most reasonable articles to appear in 1967 discussing the alienation between teacher and student, Nat Hentoff commented in *Playboy*, "Too much information has to be funneled into them so that they can go on to the 'better' colleges and then to the 'better' specialized jobs. The independent youngster with strong interests in particular areas that are not currently regarded as having a high degree of social usefulness gets in the way—particularly if he has questions for which answers are not to be found in the textbooks or the teachers at hand. He takes too much time and must either be cut to fit or leave school. He also gets in the way if his learning style is not geared to speedy achievement or predetermined tracks." [7] Hentoff's discussion, addressed to *Playboy's* mass audience rather than to the educational community, characterizes the widening public interest in the American school. Despite the general validity of Hentoff's observations, many teachers of English are well aware that the individual student deserves more attention in the English classroom and that his linguistic exploration and experiences are far more important than his accumulation of any body of facts about language or a compulsory tour through a body of recognized masterpieces. The informed teacher recognizes, however, that "individualization" is possible only when traditional patterns of classroom organization and traditional approaches to curriculum have been significantly modified. As teachers in every discipline, administrators, and the public accept the importance of individualized instruction, they are forced to consider the difficult matters of the tracking and grouping of students. Ability grouping, on the one hand, deprives every child of the rich diversity of linguistic experience which heterogeneous grouping provides. On the other, it can assist the able student to develop his intellectual and aesthetic capacities as quickly as his capabilities allow. Given the current educational structure, some grouping by ability seems inevitable in the American elementary and secondary school. Perhaps the best kind of tracking, however, is that which provides many opportunities for the student to cross from track to track for different courses and classes, even within the English curriculum. A common failing of tracking practices has been the implied assumption that the child who lacks linguistic sophistication is intellectually inferior to the child who comes to school with a rich linguistic background. The great dangers of such tracking practices in schools in disadvantaged neighborhoods are obvious.

Many of those who have provided thoughtful criticism of the schools and stressed the student's active participation in the learning process have failed to suggest concrete ways of correcting these problems. A special reading class for slow learners or for those who suffer from Dyslexia, a neurological disability which makes it difficult or impossible for the child to perceive or read accurately the symbols on the printed page, is obviously sound educational policy and not unfair grouping. For the average, the able, and the ordinary disadvantaged student, the English classroom, especially in the lower grades of the elementary school, may well offer the best opportunities for the interaction of youngsters of all backgrounds in English. No school subject can be as liberating as English if the English teacher is attuned to the needs of his students and is willing to assist them to develop their linguistic skills and the power of their imaginations through rich literary experiences. The fourth wave of curriculum reform can begin at any level when the English teacher finds ways to make his subject relevant to the lives of his students and to contemporary American society.

The Evanston Experiment

Many communities have begun programs to change traditional school patterns. One successful attempt to integrate a community through its schools and to promote individualization started in the fall of 1967 in Evanston, Illinois. A community of 79,000 persons along Lake Michigan north of Chicago, Evanston had been characterized for many years by the wealth of the majority of its citizens, the relative isolation of a growing Negro population, and a willingness to support good schools. Despite Evanston's interest in its schools and teachers, Foster School had become a Negro ghetto school while Evanston Township High School, a giant secondary school enrolling more than 4,000 students, established and maintained a national reputation for innovation and excellence. Evanston redrew its school boundaries for the first time in a generation in order to achieve the same ratio of Negro and white children in all of the elementary schools in the district. Where necessary to achieve true integration, portions of Evanston's twenty-one percent Negro student population were bussed to nearby schools. Foster, once a school for the disadvantaged, became an experimental school for the entire district. Best of all, this integration of schools was accomplished quietly and effectively, in part through the efforts of community action programs, largely because the citizens of Evanston saw that only truly integrated schools could provide rich cultural and linguistic experiences for all of Evanston's students.

The high school, which had always been integrated, adopted modular scheduling at the same time in order to meet the individual needs of students of varying abilities more effectively. Through the use of a computer, the school arranged individual programs for students based on fifteen-minute "modules" of time, modules which make it possible for classes to meet for longer or shorter periods than in ordinary schools; for students to have more time for independent study, for the use of language laboratories, for conferences with teachers, and for library work. Parenthetically one must note that the computer, programmed to sort students by sex for gym classes in the first semester, proceeded to sort them by sex for all classes. The initial confusion, then a nightmare for teachers and administrators, has since become a rich store of anecdotes. Those who planned modular scheduling for Evanston observed that traditional class scheduling—so many meetings each week for established lengths of time—failed to take into account the nature of the work which a student might be doing in a given class. A foreign language class might better meet only once or twice a week in order to allow students extra time to work in a language laboratory to develop speaking and listening skills. In English, the student needs reading time and browsing time as much as he needs discussion time in class. While modular scheduling may seem to favor the hard-working, able student who is capable of studying such advanced courses at Evanston as computer programming and Chinese, it is equally appropriate for the average or slow student who needs preparation time, teacher contact, and a sense of involvement in the educative process. But modular scheduling also places a burden on both student and teacher. The student, often not mature enough to use his newly won free time responsibly, must learn to study on his own and to use the many resources of the school available to him outside of formal classes. The teacher, accustomed to traditional ways of teaching, must adjust to a school day that is far more flexible and depends far more on personal contact between teacher and student. After a year of experience, Evanston has discovered that most students adjust quickly to the new schedule and that most teachers find the opportunity to consult more regularly with students on an individual basis extremely rewarding.

The typical elementary school in the United States has one teacher (usually a woman although more men are being attracted into teaching in the elementary grades by higher salaries, special bonuses for men with families, and the opportunity to undertake educational research in conjunction with university faculty members) in a self-contained classroom, that is, a classroom in which he may teach as many as sixteen subjects. As the knowledge explosion makes it impossible for any elementary teacher to keep pace with new developments in one field much less in many, elementary schools, especially middle schools for grades four through eight, are moving away from the self-contained classroom toward departmentalization. The child then studies with many specialists, perhaps moving from one classroom to another, perhaps remaining in one classroom into which many teachers come. Some elementary educators argue convincingly that the self-contained classroom is particularly important in the first two or three grades because of the child's need to identify with one teacher, but beyond that point the direction of American education seems to be towards departmentalization.

Moreover team-teaching, common in the good elementary school has taken much firmer hold in the secondary school than it has, for example, in the college or university. As a member of a team, the teacher must have both a thorough knowledge of his subject and the ability to work closely with his colleagues. Team-teaching, in effect, opens the long-closed classroom door and allows fellow teachers as well as students to observe the quality of a teacher's preparation and the effectiveness of his teaching. The American school teacher has resisted the "open-door classroom" for a variety of bad reasons. The college professor, probably the most vocal defender of the sanctity of his own classroom, rarely welcomes his colleagues into his classroom and almost never considers visiting a fellow professor's class. In the elementary school, particularly, but also in the high school and college, team-teaching has the special virtue of allowing teachers with a special preparation in one subject within the curriculum to share their expertise with large numbers of students. As several teachers with special knowledge work to prepare a course of study under the guidance of a master teacher, a more carefully integrated curriculum inevitably follows. In colleges, where specialists ordinarily offer only courses in their special field at the upper division level, team-teaching can improve the quality of introductory courses in literature, linguistics, and rhetoric; introduce interesting cross-disciplinary courses; encourage faculty members to discuss the techniques of effective teaching; and provide excellent teaching for large groups of students. The danger, of course, is that large classes defeat informal discussion. Programs which involve team-teaching must always provide opportunities for small groups of students to talk about books and language regularly.

Teaching on the College Campus

The chairman of a college English department, despite his keen interest in good teaching, usually knows little about the effectiveness of his department in the classroom. Even when he wishes to reward excellent teaching, he must ordinarily base his opinions upon one or two casual classroom visits, often announced in advance, upon the feedback he gets from students and faculty wives who are taking courses, upon enrollment figures, and upon that intangible quality, "the man's mind."

No subject raises more heated discussion among faculty members and administrators than the evaluation of teaching in the college or university classroom. Noting that teaching "is notoriously worse off in the universities than in the colleges," William Arrowsmith, long a spokesman for better teaching in higher education, argues that departmental power "vehemently promotes research and is hostile or indifferent to teaching. It is at the departmental level that the evaluation of teaching is subverted, since chairmen apparently equate research and teaching. . . ." [8] Unhappily, the survey on current practices in the evaluation and training of college teachers which the American Council on Education conducted in 1966 supports Professor Arrowsmith's charge: "It is clear . . . that the professor's scholarly research and publication—not information based on classroom visits, systematic student ratings, student performance on examinations, and similar sources—are currently the primary considerations in evaluating his *teaching* ability." [9] Donald D. O'Dowd goes even further, to ask indignantly, "How can a major social institution care so little about understanding its central function? It is evident that research into teaching is nonexistent in most universities and is only an incidental activity in others." [10] W. Max Wise, on the other hand, while agreeing that "Perhaps in no regard are new college teachers more deficient than in their lack of insight into the nature of the college teaching profession," believes, as I do, that a "substantial number of professors in the graduate faculties do feel an obligation to the teaching profession" and are interested in helping induct young people in the college teaching profession.[11] The critics of teaching in the universities, too, often overlook the effective teaching which is taking place on many college campuses and in many community colleges. On good, small college campuses such as Kenyon and Swarthmore, teaching matters a great deal. In such institutions, the teacher's performance in the classroom provides the primary basis for his promotions and salary increments.

Obviously, encouraging and rewarding good teaching need special attention in the large university or multiversity of today. As Allen M. Cartter notes, "excellence in teaching has gone unrewarded chiefly because we lack the means of adequate judgment. . . . We make judgments of our colleague's teaching ability, but they are largely impressions based on out-of-class contact, tinged by student comments and the occasional snatches of lecture which float over the transom." [12] Robert W. Rogers, former Head of the department at the University of Illinois and now Dean of the College of Arts and Sciences, on the other hand, believes that the skillful administrator in a college department of English of any size has access to many effective ways of evaluating the teaching of his faculty. While acknowledging that "all decisions in these matters must . . . be subjective ones, calling for the best judgment of those responsible for making them—the chairman, the full professors, the dean, and the president," Dean Rogers identifies and discusses "a number of practices which exist throughout the profession that permit a measure of objectivity in these decisions." [13] Any department will naturally discount the "Vague rumor, miscellaneous gossip, and the superficial impressions of ephemeral administrators" in favor of classroom visitations by experienced and sympathetic professors; formal and informal student polls which may supplement impressions formed during classroom visits; the evidence of ingenuity and imagination which may appear "in the kinds of textbook materials chosen, in the kinds of examinations given, in an individual's participation in professional groups devoted to the improvement of teaching, in the subjects of assigned papers and reports, in an instructor's ability to hold students in successive courses." Other evidence may be gathered from the "comparative distribution of an instructor's grades," from a "comparison of the predicted with the actual performance of students in a given class," and from "trends of enrollment in an instructor's courses." Dean Rogers finds, in short, "no lack of information about an instructor's or professor's performance in a classroom."

Thoughtful discussion of teaching in the college department of English has become more and more evident in professional journals, conferences, and conventions since 1960. It is now rare for an annual meeting of the NCTE or MLA not to include discussions of pedagogical problems in the college department, the evaluation of teaching, and the responsibility of the chairman to encourage and reward good teaching. Even as debate about the best ways to discover the good teacher and to assist the poor one grows, so do opportunities for assessing the quality of instruction in the typical college or university department of English.

Team-teaching, still used most frequently in inter-disciplinary humanities courses in the college, and television teaching, used frequently and often successfully on large campuses, have combined to inch open the classroom door on the college campus. Any of his colleagues teaching English in a college or university can learn much about effective teaching by watching a superb teacher like Walker Gibson of the University of Massachusetts on Sunrise Semester. Every secondary teacher in the 223 Nebraska high schools viewing Esther Montgomery's presentation of the Nebraska Curriculum Study Center's literature sequence for the eleventh grade could observe new ways to reach students and to challenge them. Through demonstration classrooms involving professors and teachers, the Curriculum Study and Demonstration Centers have also helped to open the teacher's classroom to his peers. In an unusual attempt to discover and reward effective teaching and to interest the department in improving classroom performance, the department of English at Western Illinois University has installed closed circuit television which enables any member of the department to observe and even to tape his own classes and those of his colleagues. Although such a practice will bring images of *1984* to the minds of some professors and denunciations of the violation of the sanctity of the classroom from others, it allows the chairman to base promotions and salary increments for good teaching on something more reliable than student polls and hearsay. More important, it commits the department to good teaching and to the establishment of a community of scholar-teachers interested as much in their classes as in their research.

The research activities of college professors of English need little defense. It is the publishing scholar who receives the awards and accolades of the profession. Even when a scholar's research subject is obscure and his articles, monographs, and books difficult to read and highly specialized, his colleagues read, admire, and make at least a casual—and often appreciative—evaluation of what he has written. Moreover, his publications give him a national audience and reputation which ally him more closely to a small number of fellow specialists than to the professors in his own department. His allegiance is to the community of scholars rather than to any one department.

Few college teachers, however, really know how well their friends and colleagues teach. As college administrations and vocal student groups demand good undergraduate and graduate teaching, departments of English must increase the number of informal and formal ways of identifying and rewarding the excellent teacher. While student ratings and prizes for excellence can certainly stimulate good teaching, they can also encourage showmanship in the classroom for its own sake and popularity contests that have little to do with good teaching or effective learning. A department chairman can recognize the importance of good teaching by opening his own classroom to his faculty and by encouraging his staff to visit, even to participate in one another's classes. In most departments at present, a chairman would encounter indifference to such a proposal or even outright hostility. At its worst, such a system could breed insecurity and enmity within a department; at its best, it might prove the existence of a real academy of students and teachers.

Innovation Comes to School and College

No single innovation introduced by a secondary school or by a college department can be nearly as significant as the effort by the Evanston community to reorganize its educational system. The changes in Evanston demonstrate both the difficulty and the possibility of large scale challenges to existing curricular and classroom patterns, school organizations, and community prejudices. In communities less determined than Evanston, the teacher of English will continue to face overcrowded classrooms, inadequate libraries, out-of-date textbooks, and even two shifts of students per day for the foreseeable future. In the face of such conditions, he can do little more now than read, study, experiment occasionally with new curriculum materials, take part in professional meetings, and help to educate his administration and community. If his chairman and principal are flexible, he may be able to introduce paperback books, tapes, and films into his classroom regularly. Even in the most conservative college departments of English, the teacher can begin to introduce a variety of media into his classes, experiment with different course organizations, and lend his support to professional meetings and articulation conferences.

When class sizes and working conditions make it possible, the teacher at any level can foster discovery on the part of his students through inductive teaching. Inductive teaching moves the teacher's desk from the front of the room and breaks up the orderly rows of pupils' chairs so that students can face one another and talk with one another and with the teacher. The lecture method, used most widely in the schools and colleges of the United States, is, of course, the only effective way to present some material to students. Teachers should reflect carefully, however, on Dr. Johnson's blunt opinion in 1766 that people have "a strange opinion that every thing should be taught by lectures. Now, I cannot see that lectures can do so much good as reading the books from which lectures are taken. I know nothing that can be best taught by lectures, except where experiments are to be shewn," an observation which he shared with company again in 1781.[5] Even asking questions in class rather than lecturing poses problems for the teacher because he is all too often looking for a particular answer to a particular question rather than attempting to stimulate discovery and discussion.

In his *Study of English Programs in Selected High Schools Which Consistently Educate Outstanding Students in English* (1966), James R. Squire learned much about what was taught in the secondary school and about how it was taught. While literature received 52.2% of the content emphasis in classroom teaching, for example, composition received 15.7% and language only 13.5%. The mass media received a bare 1.3% (p. 97). More fascinating, while teachers indicated that they spent 53.6% of their classroom time in discussion, only 14.2% in lecture, and a mere 7.0% in recitation, the expert observers in the Squire study noted that lecturing, in fact, occupied 21.1% of classroom time, simple recitation 22.2%, and discussion only 19.5% (pp. 105–106). In Professor Squire's words, "The data clearly reveal that in most schools the classrooms are teacher-dominated" (p. 105). In some classes more than in others, but particularly in English, the teacher must encourage the student to question, to respond, and to generalize from his experience and his reading rather than to memorize facts about literature and the teacher's opinions. Science and mathematics classrooms have demonstrated the effectiveness of inductive teaching. Experimenting with inductive procedures and the British notion of "talk," the English teacher must find ways to make students more responsive to literature and language. To do so, he will first have to overcome that itchy feeling which he feels when the class is not covering as much of the assigned text as the lesson plan calls for each day.

Any English teacher will be more comfortable in fostering

independent discovery in his students if he knows that they have access to an ideal "learning-center," one like that at Nova High School in Fort Lauderdale, Florida. In such a center, the customary services of the library can be extended to include slides, tapes, films, records, and even the use of the computer to assist the youngster in his studies. Private carrells allow students to listen to music, to practice speaking or listening to a foreign language, to hear lectures which they may have missed, to use the computer to solve difficult problems in mathematics and the sciences, and, one day, to be able to consult books and journals housed in libraries hundreds of miles away. In some schools, as in many colleges and graduate schools, games and case studies also help to introduce students to the complexities of such subjects as history and economics. When students can engage in such varied school and college activities, they quickly demand, as they richly deserve, an English curriculum quite different from that most common in the schools and colleges of the 1960's.

Although the best known innovations in curriculum and classroom organization have taken place in the schools, Joseph Axelrod has described important curriculum models which have been developed for higher education. In *New Patterns in Undergraduate Education: Emerging Curriculum Models for the American College* (1967), he observes that the task "of greatest priority in American higher education is the formulation of new undergraduate models for the large, urban college" and suggests that the key to a solution "appears to be the formation of 'primary groups,' that is, groups consisting of students and faculty who care about each other." [15] There must be, he urges, "new ways to combat impersonalization and isolation," not only in the residential colleges, large and small, but in community colleges as well. Ironically enough, as Allan M. Cartter has noted, while the community college is demonstrating that a successful college program can be offered to a wide range of students within a large urban area, the senior college and the university are "rediscovering the value of collegiate residence just at the time when the national trend is toward the student's living at home." Cartter argues "that two-thirds of the value of attending college is the residential experience: the loosening of ties with family and community, and the consequent broadening of intellectual horizons and cultural traditions." Because "New conditions demand the reorganization of the disciplines," new curriculum models "are responding to these conditions" by trying to avoid too early specialization and continued fragmentation of the disciplines. Calling for interdisciplinary programs, community involvement programs, and international education, Axelrod praises the "hundred campuses which have community involvement programs in one form or another" and urban institutions in which "the city itself is used in a systematic way as an educational laboratory" As institutional leaders such as Yale deemphasize grading and as students call for and are granted more participation in course planning, a "new view of teaching and learning as an engagement in joint inquiry" is replacing "old patterns of authority and status." In 1967 alone, for example, one could point to such programs as the "Voice Project" at Stanford University, an experimental writing program using creative writers to help Stanford freshmen study the relationship of the spoken voice to the particular "voice" discernible in good prose; the Harvard University Expository Writing Program, which enabled talented freshmen and upperclassmen to study the relationship between writing and the demands of particular disciplines; and the "Thirteen Colleges Project," an attempt to restructure the entire academic program for some 1250 Negro college freshmen.

Although he is concerned with the entire college curriculum, Axelrod offers a direct challenge to those English departments which cling to the notion that they are preparing only college majors and young Ph.D.'s in the literary heritage of England and of the United States. His criticisms extend to the diminishing number of departments which still restrict the study of language to the reading of Beowulf and Chaucer and to the history of the language, consider advanced composition appropriate only for the prospective secondary school teacher, and view courses in creative writing as luxuries to be used to attract writers to campuses for a semester or an academic year. Axelrod would call for more and better courses for the non-major in English, the student whom Harold Martin places in "the commonwealth of the college or university," the student who wishes to study literature as a broadening, humane experience.[16] He is still too often excluded from the challenging advanced courses in the English department because of rigid college or departmental regulations; because the department, often the largest in the college, is overburdened and understaffed and must concentrate its attention on its majors; and because some departments wish to discourage the dilettante. Because this student, majoring in chemistry, engineering or business, may benefit most from the humanizing experience of language and literature in our pragmatic, materialistic society, college departments of English should use their size and influence on the campus to attract him.

Such a broadening of the interests of the college department should not be viewed as an attack on the integrity of the discipline or a watering-down of standards. The chairman, of course, may lose sleep worrying about the problems of staffing and funding so many programs within his department and will have to decide how far his resources will stretch in any one year. He must, however, guarantee that his full professors do not withdraw like mandarins, as institutions of higher learning are "altered as vastly by the new information sciences as they were five centuries ago . . . by the advent of an earlier technology, which is known as printing." [17] If college departments thoughtfully redefine the nature of their subject and develop pedagogical strategies which incorporate the new information sciences, they can play a more important role in the "fact and dollar" society of the 1970's than they have ever played before.

One step toward the redefinition of the role of English in the college or university can be taken by employing poets, dramatists, novelists, or essayists to teach courses while they continue to practice their art. The fresh look at curriculum which the writer can bring to the department and the dialogue about the goals of English teaching among scholars, teachers, and writers cannot fail to enliven the college department. The writer-teacher has become a familiar figure to the college department of English. His greatest contribution to students and his colleagues may be that he "knows, in a way that others perhaps cannot, the particularity of the creative act, the necessity to find within any project its own determining principles. He alone can know what the process of writing entails, that combination of conscious memory and unconscious discovery, of knowledge and craft and vision and work and chance and critical detachment. And certainly his own experience, his success or lack of it, can be instructive as well as comforting." [18] While some writers, like Robert Creeley at the State University of New York at Buffalo or Karl Shapiro at the Chicago Circle Campus of the University of Illinois, are permanent members of their departments, most writers, either with or without academic backgrounds, come to the college campus for an evening, a week, or even a semester or academic year to talk about their writing, to consult with student writers, and to teach courses in "creative writing." Despite the growing number of special, separate programs in creative writing, Richard Scowcroft urges that the writer-in-residence become an integral part of the English department: "It is desirable to keep writing—imaginative as well as expository— within the confines of the English department and to accept the assumption that the study of past as well as present literature, even of genres and styles remote from those the writing students favor, cannot harm their writing and may actually help it." [19] Within the department, the writer should be encouraged to teach a variety of courses in literature and in composition; he should not be tucked away in a corner of the department designed exclusively for courses in "creative writing." By contrast, Reed Whittemore would remove the writer from the English department and place him in other departments within the college to demonstrate "that the language of facts and the language of feelings, of science and literature, of the self and the other, or even of prose and poetry are not finally separable." [20] Whittemore wants the writer on campus to have "intellectual experiences, that is, academic experiences outside English in the various other shops on the campus" both because of "the value of non-literary surroundings for the production of literary things" and because these experiences can help to break down the barriers which separate the disciplines.

To encourage writers to seek academic appointments and to suggest the many roles a writer can play in the department, the National Endowment for the Arts granted matching funds to the MLA and the American Center of P.E.N. early in 1968 to initiate discussion about the place of the writer on the college campus. Reed Whittemore, Robert Creeley, Fredson Bowers, John Gerber, and others who met in New York in February agreed quickly that critic and practitioner together could profitably experiment with new ways of teaching English. If the writer is treated as a member of the university community rather than as a curiosity on loan to teach "creative writing" to a handful of students, he can become a key to the revitalization of the undergraduate curriculum in English.

Most, perhaps the majority of, college English teachers are unaware of the sweeping changes that have taken place in the best elementary and secondary schools and junior and community colleges. For some college faculty members innovation is a television lecture, the introduction of a trimester, a paperback book library in the department, or team-teaching in a humanities program which incorporates records, slides, and films as well as books. The American college and university and the department of English face more fundamental changes than these in the next decade. Michigan State University, for example, pioneered among the large state universities in 1961 by establishing "living-learning residence halls" which help combat the depersonalization which the multiversity can so easily engender. By 1967, more than 11,000 students had been distributed among nine residential "colleges" within the university. In these smaller communities, students and faculty members can know one another well and enjoy the advantages of the smaller college at the same time that they have access to the resources of a great university. The department of English at the University of Illinois, encouraged by the administration to find ways to reach the individual student within the immense university community, has brought the freshman English course to the student's dormitory so that he may attend class and study with those whom he knows well. As more and more universities encourage students to spend a year abroad, individual departments must offer courses which are relevant to the needs and interests of these new citizens of the world. The professor who is teaching literature to Stanford students in California one quarter and in Spain or Germany the next must have an understanding of literary works beyond the scope of British and American literature. Despite the adjustments in departmental organization and in curriculum which such programs as these have already required, the college and university community has only begun to feel the effects of the junior college movement, computerization, sophisticated information retrieval systems, the curriculum reforms of the 1960's, society's demands on education, and television and other mass media.

In the 1970's, the junior college movement will force almost every college department of English in the United States to find the answers to several important questions. Graduate departments must ask how they can continue to prepare Ph.D.'s for the colleges and universities and still train the 6,000 junior college teachers of English already needed. If the junior colleges are to assume the responsibility for seventy-five percent of the lower division college courses in English by 1975, graduate English departments in the universities must establish programs which will provide relevant supervised practice teaching for prospective college teachers. The graduate department must also ask whether the community college, which will soon be educating by far the largest share of the college population, will seriously diminish the amount of financial support available for graduate research and teaching. If it cannot demonstrate that it continues to perform major public services, that it is concerned with crucial social problems, and that its humanistic activities are vital to American intellectual life, the graduate department of English will find it difficult to obtain the continuing support of alumni and of those state and federal programs designed to aid higher education. The college department, into whose upper-division courses junior college students will flow each fall, must ask how effectively it is able to integrate these students into its programs for the major and for the teaching major in English. It must ask itself, furthermore, how well it can survive the loss of its principal source of strength on the campus, its tremendous freshman and sophomore composition and introductory literature courses. The quality of the articulation which takes place between the junior college English teacher and the professor of

English in the next few years will determine not only the shape of English instruction in higher education in the 1970's but the viability and vitality of the college and university department of English.

The Electronic Revolution

In his enlightened discussion of the impact of the computer on modern society, Edmund Farrell observes, "Although the electronic revolution is occurring because a complex of media— radio, film, television, tape recorder, phonograph, and record among them—have become integral to our lives, the rate of the revolution seems proportional to the production of computers." [21] This electronic revolution, "the inexorable force transforming not only education but the whole of society," has barely touched the department of English. Major universities and large school systems have been using computers for a variety of purposes, including student record keeping, for more than a decade and smaller institutions have now begun to employ them. Late in 1966, for example, Franklin and Marshall College in Lancaster, Pennsylvania, announced plans for a giant computer center which would link together fifty Middle Atlantic area colleges and research institutions. The two hundred remote stations in the computer network will enable humanists as well as scientists to explore new uses for the computer in teaching and research. The impressive results of James R. Squire's study of selected high school English departments also suggest how effectively the computer can help the university scholar to process large masses of raw data. Scholars working with university funds and with grants from the American Council of Learned Societies have also demonstrated that the computer can assist the scholar in the collation of texts and preparation of scholarly editions. Despite such achievements and Peter Schrag's wry proclamation that "The message is that the computer is coming: the Messenger is The Industry, and the gospel prophecy is Revolution in the Classroom," the college community honestly does not yet know how deeply and in what ways the computer will change higher education in the humanities.[22] Schrag observes that most of the educational industry's "output is still relatively conventional textbooks, study guides, films, projectors, workbooks, tests, micro-films, classroom weeklies, and programmed materials printed on paper and not on computer tape." Noting the lack of "any large body of tested material for computer or for any other new technological device," Schrag lays the blame squarely on the educators, including college teachers of English: "More important for the future is the relative unwillingness of the education establishment to make changes on its own initiative." The result of this inertia, Schrag concludes, is more of an asset to the electronics industry than a barrier: "The demonstrated inadequacies of the schools—and especially in the most visible disaster areas (in the slums, for example) provide an opening for the entrepreneur." Reporting that, while seventy-five percent of all undergraduates are enrolled in courses in which a computer would be very useful, fewer than five percent of the students have adequate access to such machines, *Time* magazine (19 May 1967) warned, "If the computer is really going to revolutionize education, the colleges are going to have to develop more flexible and sophisticated approaches to programmed instruction—and the Federal Government is going to have to decide whether it wants to put its money behind the computer as a teaching as well as a research tool." The implications for the college professor of English are great. Before the electronics industry can ask the teacher, "What can you do that the machine can't?", the college teacher must educate himself to the potentials of the computer and consider how it and other technological innovations can assist him in his research and in his teaching. Recognizing the limitations of any programmed instruction in English, he must still acknowledge the assistance which the computer can offer. Its ability to store and sort immense quantities of information can save the scholar numberless hours. Its ability to share information with teachers and students in many locations at once automatically increases the size and strength of a college library. Through its graduate programs, fellowships, and research grants, the university department of English must educate a cadre of specialists in English who can devise creative uses for the computer in the humanities. Before the 1970's have passed some knowledge of computer capability and programming may well be considered an essential part of the education of every potential college professor of English.

The MLA, the NCTE, and the Linguistic Society of America launched one of the most ambitious computer-assisted information retrieval systems in the entire field of the humanities in 1967. In a period of three years, the associations will develop a compatible scholarly and pedagogical bibliography in English and the modern foreign languages. Under the general supervision of the MLA bibliographer, Harrison Meserole of Pennsylvania State University, and of the NCTE bibliographer, Nathan S. Blount of the University of Wisconsin, teams of experts will prepare yearly bibliographies in linguistics, scholarly research in English and the modern foreign languages, foreign language pedagogy at all levels of education, and English pedagogy from the elementary school through the graduate school. The 20,814 items which were included in the *PMLA International Bibliography* published in 1967 indicate the scope of the project. By the early 1970's, scholars and teachers will be able to obtain bibliographical citations in any of these areas and annotations for every citation. As each year's bibliographies are punched onto computer tape, any teacher of English will be able to retrieve a cumulative, annotated bibliography of, say, scholarly and pedagogical articles on *Julius Caesar*. It is technologically possible even now, although cumulative, compatible, annotated bibliographies in English are not yet available, for a teacher in his school or a professor in his college library to use a remote station to request a computer hundreds of miles away to retrieve the citations for all articles on the teaching of *Julius Caesar* to adolescents written between 1958 and 1968. Having reviewed the list produced by the computer, he might next request annotations of approximately 200 words in length for particularly interesting articles. If the annotations identified some articles as unusually stimulating or provocative, he might then request print-outs of those items. When the multi-volume *London Stage* is punched onto computer tape and properly programmed, any scholar will be able to discover in a matter of minutes how often George Farquhar's *Recruiting Officer* was played in the eighteenth century, where it was played, and who played Sergeant Kite.

These aids to the scholar and teacher are not yet realities. They suggest, however, how important a resource tool the computer can be for the English teacher. Few teachers, unfortunately, have yet discovered creative ways to use the computer in the day-by-day activities of the English classroom. Donald Suppes of Stanford University is an exception. Using an IBM 1510 series to teach mathematics and reading through the computer to disadvantaged youngsters in the Brentwood School in Palo Alto, he has demonstrated how computer programmed instruction can help students master basic skills.[23] The Suppes program, which has been widely publicized as a pilot for future programs, leads youngsters through 180 reading lessons in the first grade in the hopes of helping them develop third grade reading skills in one year. The complex equipment—an image projector with random selection of 1000 frames on 16 mm. film, a four track tape recorder for each child (two for messages to the child, a third to allow the child to record, and a fourth for control purposes), a television screen or scope, a light pen, and a typewriter—take the student from sound, pictures, and word clues to word recognition and provide remedial work if necessary. The children at Brentwood, who work at the computer stations for about twenty minutes at a time, even have specially constructed chairs which allow them to swivel freely and quietly. Watching the youngsters learning to read, one is immediately caught by their interest and enthusiasm. The adult who takes the introductory lessons, based on a linguistic approach to reading, finds himself impressed by the sophistication of the machines and of the programs and by the individual attention which the program makes possible for each learner. Whenever the student makes a mistake, the machine patiently leads him through another of its five tracks to help him master the lesson. In addition, the teacher, who can monitor any station, is constantly available to counsel individual students, to offer them reassurance, and to reenforce what they have learned.

Such an elaborate program is obviously expensive. The purchase price of the sophisticated equipment approaches half a million dollars. On a monthly rental basis the actual cost of instruction is about $200.00 per unit for each of sixteen outlets, still a prohibitive amount for all but the largest and wealthiest schools. When a school can move students through the program at approximately half-hour intervals throughout the school day, however, the cost of instruction is about the same as hiring remedial reading teachers to give individual attention to the youngsters. If the Suppes experimental program successfully helps children to read more quickly than they would in the conventional classroom, then computer-assisted instruction in English may well prove equally valuable for the slow reader in high school or college and for the student struggling to master a standard dialect. If the program does motivate students to work successfully on their own and still allows teachers to provide special, individual attention to students, then it warrants the high expense of equipment rental. The computer can help the student build skills just as it helps the teacher obtain scholarly and pedagogical information or undertake certain kinds of research. The fundamental question still to be answered is whether literary studies can or should be programmed. Because the literary response is essentially a personal one, one must ask how appropriate programmed instruction can ever be in a humanistic study which demands talk, discussion, and response. Like the book or the film, the computer is a fact of contemporary life. What use college professors of English make of it in the next decade is an important, unanswered question.

New curriculums, new patterns of school organization, and new media only serve education insofar as they motivate students to learn and provide them with valuable, challenging learning experiences. When English classes fail to interest students despite the most thoughtful curriculum planning, the English teacher who insists on divorcing the content of English from the world of experience available to the student outside of class may well be to blame. No one would argue that the English teacher should cater to the lowest popular level of culture. However, the English classroom *is* an appropriate place for the introduction of materials and the discussion of ideas relevant to the lives of students. Motion pictures, television, and records are integral parts of the experience of every student. To ignore them in a class concerned with the uses of language is foolhardy. Global television has made immediate to even the casual observer the most momentous as well as the most trivial events. At its best, television can bring the experience of drama into even the most impoverished home. A record album such as *Sgt. Pepper's Lonely Hearts Club Band* not only attracts a mass audience but, in the opinion of Tom Phillips, turns "the record-album itself into an art form, and a form that works." [24] As John M. Culkin, S.J., of Fordham University, observes, "Motion pictures are communicating with this generation because they are *emotion* pictures, because they deal with experience. . . . The values of human communication and understanding should be given priority over all the high rhetoric about art." [25] Even the lowly television commercial or advertisement in a slick magazine present the student with extraordinarily effective uses of language. The student who enters the English classroom has been bombarded with sights and sounds from the moment he arose in the morning. In the English class he has an opportunity to examine the uses of language in his society and the ways in which the media attempt to manipulate his emotions and his opinions. If the English teacher ignores the opportunity to discuss the uses of language in the media in order to teach one more poem by William Wordsworth, he has reduced English in modern society to an irrelevancy. Poetry, novels, stories, essays, and plays have a central part in any English curriculum because they help the student learn how language can be used to order and to intensify experience. The teacher must also find room for television, the film, and other media. These media are the language in action which affects the student of today.

If the schools and especially the colleges have not used media well, neither have they produced media for the classroom. The kinescopes and films made for students and teachers of English have generally been shockingly poor. The reliance on reproducing the lecture, the general low quality of camera work, the lack of imagination, and the shamefully inadequate budgets which these productions make apparent are another indication of how slow the English profession has been to incorporate media into the classroom. Jerrold Zacharias, the guiding force behind the PSSC films produced by Educational Services, Incorporated, has pointed out that effective classroom films are expensive, that they require a professional technical competence which the scholar-teacher does not possess, and that they can be incredibly useful as a teaching device. At a cost of approximately one thousand dollars per running minute, the films he has produced for the schools should be good—and they are. In the social sciences, too, such films as the documentary on the life of the Eskimo indicate how professionally ESI has approached filmmaking.

The fourteen kinescopes produced by the Commission on English during the early 1960's are not without merit. The enthusiasm of the lecturers and the quality of their commentary on literature, language, and rhetoric almost redeem the painful inadequacies of the camera work and of the editing. The films produced by the NCTE for elementary teachers in 1967 again suggest the lack of commitment to the effective use of media characteristic of the English profession. To provide consultants with almost no time to work before the camera, to use the camera almost entirely to record another lecture, and to attempt to produce dozens of films on an insufficient budget assure a series largely unremarkable and undistinguished. One does not expect the school and college English teacher to produce films which rival *Gone With the Wind* or television programs as professional as *Gunsmoke*, but he should concern himself more directly with the use and production of distinguished films for the English classroom.

Many commercial films are currently available for classroom use. Of special interest, perhaps is Robert Lowell's *Benito Cereno*, produced by the National Educational Television network. Other films which have been used successfully in the classroom include *Yankee Painter, Jack Levine, Faulkner's Mississippi, Dickens's England,* and *Nothing But a Man.* The *United States Literature* series produced by NET and the Esso Repertory Theatre are excellent examples of series appropriate for the school and college English classroom. The profession has tried to inform teachers about films which are especially appropriate for the English classroom, to educate them to the use of film as an integral rather than a peripheral part of the English curriculum, and to commission and participate in the development of films and kinescopes of high quality. The book is in no danger in the English classroom when the teacher and his students view a film, watch a play, or study the language of television. Still, one teacher in a large secondary school, upon learning that she would be reading a play with her students to prepare them for a live performance, wondered, "How much time will all this take from English?" Teachers will continue to ask such questions until institutes, conventions, inservice workshops, and the publications of the profession convince English teachers that media are essential to the English classroom in the years ahead.

The Slowness of Change

The English teacher in a large school district or a multiversity faces enormous difficulties if he tries to change the English curriculum. The search for excellence takes place amidst the inertia of some administrators and political machines, the reluctance of many taxpayers to support expensive new programs, and the inadequacies of many overcrowded, ill-equipped, and demoralized schools. Despite real efforts to improve the teaching of English in many Chicago schools, Philip Hauser brands the huge Chicago public school system (600,000 students in 600 buildings taught by 23,000 teachers) "a giant of inertia, inequity, injustice, intransigence, and trained incapacity." [26] Charles and Bonnie Rensberg blame Mayor Richard Daley for convincing "the business community that Chicago could get quality education at bargain-counter rates." [27] Such accusations fail to do justice to the incredibly complex problems faced by major school districts. Population shifts; the education of many different kinds of disadvantaged youngsters; the search for funds to improve salaries and working conditions for teachers, build needed facilities, and establish and maintain experimental curriculum projects and inservice programs; changing technologies; and the establishment of racially integrated schools which provide educational opportunities for all kinds of pupils are sufficient to tax the imagination and resources of any administration. As Chicago's superintendent of schools, James Redmond, plans a billion-dollar program to establish education parks in the city, many teachers of English will have to face new teaching situations and conditions at the same time that they try to evaluate and incorporate into their teaching new curriculum models in English. Superintendent Redmond has planned to build huge campus-like complexes which draw students from large areas of the city and offer education from preschool through high school. Special model schools, middle schools for grades five through eight, and school-home preschool centers designed for low income neighborhoods will tax the resources of the city and of the individual teacher of English. Even as the public schools plan for integration and quality in education, the city's junior colleges have been reorganized and strengthened under the Illinois state master plan for higher education and the Chicago Circle Campus of the University of Illinois has blossomed into a major institution offering both undergraduate and graduate work. The educational system of the city of Chicago, like that of such other cities as New York, Philadelphia, Detroit, and Washington, D.C., is in the process of tremendous change. The English teacher caught up in that change at the school or college level must respond by developing new skills and acquiring new knowledge. Most of all, he will have to prove himself flexible as the traditional, comfortable, familiar classroom in the neighborhood school is challenged and changed.

In the period of transition before major reforms in the educational systems of the cities force the English teacher to redefine his role, he may find his task changing, growing more difficult, often becoming more frustrating in the inner-city school. If he has been teaching in an older neighborhood school, he watches the plant decline, the neighborhood change, and discipline become the major concern of the faculty. Red tape and inadequate funds make the use of projectors and phonographs difficult, if not impossible. If violence is in the neighborhood, it enters the school as well. The honors class in English which was once his pride becomes a class in English as a second language. He watches novice teachers come and go more and more rapidly as the school declines. Only his own dedication remains constant.

Other major cities in the United States, also criticized roundly for the inadequacies of their schools, have planned reforms as sweeping and as controversial as the Chicago plan. An advisory committee appointed by Mayor John Lindsay recommended in 1967 that New York City's gigantic school system be divided into thirty to sixty largely autonomous and locally governed school districts. Although New York's State Legislature failed to take any firm action in 1968, the plan would establish parent-dominated school boards to run community school districts, have the authority to employ school personnel, determine educational policy, and spend funds allocated by the city of New York. The bold restructuring of the nation's largest school system proposed by the Mayor's committee, headed by McGeorge Bundy, is one of several attempts to give vitality to a school system marked by overcrowding, many substandard facilities, a huge disadvantaged student population, and vocal parent and community groups demanding the right to help set educational policies. While politics, finances, and differing philosophies of public education spark controversies which will keep substantive change from coming to New York's schools quickly, the English teacher may well find himself trying to teach language and literature to some of those 40,000 students in New York schools who speak no English at all.

In the meantime, inspired teachers like Mary Finocchiaro of Hunter College have developed teaching materials and techniques which develop language skills in mixed classes of Spanish-speaking, Negro, and other children in the New York system. The methodology which she has developed for teaching English and Spanish simultaneously to primary-grade students stimulates Spanish-speaking children to learn English even as it helps English-speaking children to communicate in Spanish. The teacher who wishes to reach the adolescents who crowd into the secondary schools of New York needs the programs and advice of such curriculum specialists as Marjorie Smiley and Daniel Fader. More even than the English teacher in a prosperous suburban community, the urban teacher needs the inservice work in linguistics and the time for thoughtful curriculum planning which the overcrowded city school is least likely to be able to provide.

In 1967, Washington, D.C., with its dominant Negro student population, abolished the tracking system which grouped youngsters according to ability. Those educators who opposed the tracking system argued that such grouping segregates the disadvantaged child into classes for slow learners, places him in overcrowded and substandard school buildings, and offers him the least competent and least experienced teachers in the public school system. The call for an end to culturally-loaded placement and achievement tests and for the assignment of a system's best-qualified teachers to schools which need attention most desperately is being echoed in every major city in the United States.

The non-graded elementary school, which now exists in nearly one third of the larger school systems in the nation, is one pattern of school organization which can help to modify rigid tracking. The child who is allowed to move on to the equivalent of a third-grade reading class while he continues to work in a second-grade arithmetic class has escaped some of the rigid compartmentalization which characterizes many school programs. Experiments with the curriculum, with technology, with new kinds of inservice programs for inner-city teachers, and with special programs for the linguistically and culturally disadvantaged have become an accepted part of the activities of school districts throughout the United States. Not only the published reports of the NCTE Committee on Promising Practices in the Teaching of English but the hundreds of manuscripts submitted to the committee over the past five years testify to the vitality of the American school system and of the teacher of English. By 1964 teachers, administrators, consultants, and representatives of community agencies had begun to establish special programs in the elementary schools of Sacramento, California, for children from different cultural backgrounds. In Pittsburgh, Schenley High School, in which more than half of the students come from culturally disadvantaged homes, has established special programs to correct substandard speech patterns and set up demonstration classrooms for the entire city system. Educational television brings language and linguistics to thousands of fourth and fifth graders in Cincinnati and American literature to students in Philadelphia and Detroit. In Lewis County, New York, talented youngsters living in relatively isolated areas have been being brought together for special cultural activities for more than a decade while five Colorado schools use conference telephone facilities to bring expert teaching to children in widely separated small schools. Education in 1968 is already a kaleidoscope of innovation and experimentation across the country.[28] The gift of the 1970's will be the easier and more regular exchange of information about successful curriculum reforms.

ERIC

The regular bibliographies prepared by the MLA and NCTE will be one means of facilitating this exchange. The information programs and demonstration classrooms set up by the Regional Educational Laboratories and by the Research and Development Centers established under Title IV of the Elementary and Secondary Education Act of 1965 will also promote the dissemination of information about promising school programs. Institute programs funded by the Education Professions Development Act will bring school and college teachers, teacher trainers and administrators together to exchange ideas and projects. Most important for the regular, widespread dissemination of information about research in education, however, will be the facilities of the fledgling Educational Resources Information Centers. Established by the Office of Education in 1967, the English ERIC Centers provide information about significant current reports, articles, monographs, speeches, and books for the profession and make these materials readily available at extremely low cost through the ERIC Document Reproduction Service. Although only twenty ERIC clearinghouses serve the entire area of education, three cover the immense field of English. The NCTE clearinghouse collects and disseminates research reports and other documents relevant to all aspects of the teaching of English from kindergarten through the twelfth grade, the preparation of teachers of English for the schools, the preparation of specialists in English Education and in the teaching of English. The MLA clearinghouse is concerned with the undergraduate and graduate program in English, including introductory composition, general education, the English major, and the preparation of teachers of English for two- and four-year colleges and universities. The clearinghouse sponsored by the Center for Applied Linguistics deals with English for speakers of other languages, the teaching of standard English to speakers of nonstandard English, and applied linguistics. These clearinghouses, now feeding nearly one hundred documents a month into a national information retrieval system, coordinate their activities with other clearinghouses in such related areas as the problems of the disadvantaged, the two-year college, and reading. Not only can ERIC make information about curriculum innovation available to large numbers of teachers and administrators very quickly, but it can generate discussion and further research. Each clearinghouse has funds to commission, for example, "state of the art" papers which allow distinguished scholars to survey the major research in an important area of the curriculum, to evaluate what has been done, and to make recommendations for further needed research. Through ERIC too, the English teacher has easy access to hundreds of unpublished documents which would otherwise remain difficult to obtain and can correlate vast amounts of data which may reveal significant trends in education. English teachers, school principals, curriculum planners, and state supervisors of English have never before had the prospect of access to so much material.

Critics of the ERIC system have noted that in its first two years documents were difficult to locate in the monthly publication of abstracts, *Research in Education,* issued by central ERIC. They have wondered, too, whether the clearinghouses would be able to locate worthwhile studies to include in the central system and in their local files. Does not, some asked, all good research find publication on its own? The answer, of course, is no. Many small studies which can affect the teaching of English in school or college never reach a wide audience. ERIC promises a service to English which will grow in importance throughout the 1970's. As more innovation takes place, as more school systems experiment with new curriculum materials and new teaching techniques, as university departments of English take a more active role in American public education, the rapid and regular exchange of information becomes of primary importance. Not only will there never be a sufficient number of journals to print substantive articles and research reports, but no teacher or professor will ever have a sufficient amount of time to read or even scan the great flow of information which is already a hallmark of the English profession. The network of ERIC clearinghouses can become the indispensable research assistant for every teacher of English.

Censorship
As ERIC and the great bibliographical services now being planned make it possible for teachers of English in the schools and colleges to share the results of significant research and to strengthen the sense of an English community in the United States, the English teacher can become a more vigorous intellectual force in American public life. While the teacher should not exercise his position of leadership in the school or community irresponsibly, he has special competence to address himself to certain issues and problems which plague our society. Censorship is a crucially important one. The flood of pornography which citizens' groups observe in bookstores and on magazine racks prompts only the more obvious kinds of censorship. More subtle and more dangerous are the pressures exerted by political and even racial groups. Responding to public outcry about pornography, President Johnson established an eighteen-man Commission on Obscenity and Pornography under public law 90-100 in October 1967. The Commission has been charged with evaluating and recommending definitions of obscenity and pornography, with ascertaining the methods employed in the distribution of obscene and pornographic materials, and with exploring the nature and volume of traffic in such materials in order to recommend legislative, administrative, or other advisable and appropriate action to the president and to the Congress. Because the charge to this Commission is so important to the future right of the individual to choose what he shall read and think, more than twenty organizations, led by the NCTE and the American Library Association, organized a National Committee on the Freedom to Learn late in 1967 to offer counsel to the president's Commission and

to guarantee to the American public that it operates as more than a clearinghouse for those who would inhibit intellectual freedom, including the right to read. Because attacks on intellectual freedom are so widespread in the United States, the New Jersey Committee on the Right to Read, joined by associations in Maryland, New York, and Illinois, and with letters of inquiry from more than thirty other states, is forming a national association of interested laymen to work with teachers and public officials to extend and defend the right of intellectual freedom. Teachers of English have a moral obligation to participate in local and national efforts to control the censors.

Parents and other citizens in cities throughout the country naturally become alarmed about the state of public morality when they are exposed to violence in their own streets, new statistics on the rising crime rate in the United States, and pictures and stories on television and in the newspapers and weekly magazines which depict a lawless, sexually-oriented society. English teachers and school administrators encounter censorship most directly in attempts by individual parents and parent and community groups to remove from required reading lists books which have been assigned for class study. Sometimes the objections which parents raise indicate a more responsible approach to the curriculum than an inexperienced teacher has taken. Sometimes, too, parents simply wish to be informed about the goals which the teacher has set for his class. At its best, the interest exhibited by individuals and by parent groups demonstrates a close working relationship between the school and the community. When the teacher has the support of his administration and can provide a thoughtful rationale for the inclusion of the books in question, he can often convince those who have registered an objection that the books should remain in the curriculum. When he finds himself under attack, he must consider those alternatives for action which he discussed in his teacher preparation program. From the NCTE, from state groups, from the American Library Association, and from the Civil Liberties Union he can obtain support. Before censorship arises, he and his colleagues should have established regular procedures for selecting and reviewing books which will be required of or suggested to students.

Perhaps even more dangerous than the overt censorship which can be fought in the press and in the public forum is the hidden censorship which leads teachers to omit books from their courses from fear of attack, librarians to forget or neglect to order books for school and public libraries, and owners of bookstores and newsstands to remove titles under the pressures exerted by parents, fellow merchants, and representatives of extremist groups. Such covert censorship may keep the English teacher and his school "safe" and may protect the businessman from economic reprisals, but it diminishes the free exchange of ideas in a democratic society. These remarks are not a defense of hard-core pornography in drugstores frequented by adolescents in every community, but a plea for the right of free inquiry, a right which many American schools and cities are in danger of losing. The NCTE, in two important monographs, makes an eloquent plea for the free exchange of ideas. In *Obscenity, the Law, and the English Teacher* (1966), James R. Squire explains that teachers of English "share with others a concern lest the free exchange of ideas in school and college, no less than in American society as a whole, be restricted by irresponsible efforts to limit access to controversial books. They share with parents an obligation to help young people cope with ideas, to distinguish the valid from the invalid, develop standards for discrimination. And they share the responsibility of introducing these readers to some of the great literary works of American culture, many of which present controversial ideas and images with all the richness and power of language that the great artist can command." [29] Robert Hogan notes that the real harm in reading such a controversial student favorite as J. D. Salinger's *The Catcher in the Rye* "is not in the reading of it (and we must assume most adolescents will read it). The harm comes from reading it in isolation without the chance to discuss it with other students and without a sensitive teacher or another adult who can make clear that it is not a dirty book, even though it repeats four times one of the most tabu (and, incidentally, most widely used) words in English, and even though it includes a vivid scene with a prostitute. It is at heart a book which pleads for compassion in an age that can surely use compassion, but for some students this point comes out only in discussion." [30] In an essay written as much for parents and school administrators as for teachers of English, Hogan recommends that teachers "devise programs in literature and programs of public action that take into account the maturing nature of adolescents, the broad world of accessible reading which sifts through the coarse screen constructed by the Supreme Court, and the world itself—programs which do not rest on the hope of a germ-free environment in a germ-ridden world."

Testing and Ability Grouping

The selection, administration, evaluation, and use of tests and examinations are as fundamental to the English teacher's success in the classroom as his opposition to both overt and covert censorship. In schools which include large numbers of students from migrant families, those for whom standard English is a second language or dialect, and those who come from culturally and economically deprived homes, testing and tracking become classroom and community problems. The culturally loaded standardized tests which have proliferated in the schools discriminate against the disadvantaged youngster by measuring more his acculturation to middle class society than his native intelligence. Although the test makers are constantly working to reduce the cultural and linguistic bias of standardized tests, many bright students still find themselves relegated to classes for slow learners and to teachers ill-equipped to instruct students who are not slow but different from the white, middle-class child. In his discussion of "the 100 million standardized tests given annually in the nation's elementary and high schools as well as several million college entrance and scholarship exams," Hillel Black protests against the "Great Sorting" which "begins near the end of the elementary school or the beginning of the ninth grade" and affects every pupil.[31] He argues further that "many young people in the United States are being penalized because of the overemphasis by some test makers on the merchandising of tests and the ignorance of many school officials." Mass testing, he suggests, "has frequently become a means of exclusion instead of an aid in helping children make the best possible choice for their own future." Sociologist David Goslin identifies even more fundamental social effects of testing and tracking in *The Search for Ability:* "In addition to the visible effects of being placed in a special class or getting the best job, a high or low test score may have the less obvious impact of raising or lowering self-esteem, altering the level of aspiration, and thereby changing the individual's achievement motivation." [32]

The entire area of testing, internally by classroom teachers through quizzes, papers, and examinations, and externally through school-wide, system-wide, state, and national examinations, needs the careful study which the Dartmouth Seminar called for in 1966. If, for example, tests and examinations influence curriculum planning and the nature of the English program in a school, they can impair the efforts of dedicated, qualified teachers of English who are specially responsive to the needs of disadvantaged students. In a nation that prizes statistics and polls, schools must not penalize children by scoring them too often and by occupying precious classroom time with batteries of repetitive achievement tests which do little more than swell student record folders with raw data which overworked guidance counselors and teachers have neither time nor competence to interpret. Properly administered and carefully analyzed diagnostic tests can provide the English teacher with useful information about the reading level and the general linguistic sophistication of his students. Such tests can identify the student who needs individual attention, or a reading specialist, or the opportunity to read widely on his own. Poorly used, diagnostic tests and achievement tests classify students artificially and program them into ability groupings for which they may be neither intellectually nor emotionally suited. Some school administrations and school boards have even concluded that the quality of an individual school or of an entire school system can be measured by the number of external examinations which are administered each year. Other schools and systems, anxious to impress parents and taxpayers with the quality of the education which they are providing, use school time not for learning but for cramming for examinations. Education in the best British schools, now escaping from the "eleven plus" examination which determined the course of a student's entire life before he had become an adolescent, have urged American scholars and teachers to examine the impact of testing on students very carefully before relying upon examinations regularly and heavily. The English teacher, particularly, must recognize that the ability groupings which testing so often leads to deprive youngsters of every background from the rich linguistic experiences which come from heterogeneous grouping. In the English classroom, at least, students must form an intellectual and cultural community which takes little cognizance of test scores and achievement records. Until the rote learning of facts about language and literature upon which ill-prepared teachers of English have relied is replaced by new curriculum patterns, new techniques for reaching students, and professionally qualified teachers, no such community will be possible. Moreover, until the American public school and college redefine their role in modern society and their educational goals, testing, grouping, and the attendant ills they reflect will characterize American education.

Throughout the 1960's, English teachers, their colleagues in other disciplines, and the principals and deans who administer our schools and colleges have accepted educational innovation with reluctance. The easy flow of information about curriculum change, technology, new standards for teacher preparation programs, and widely publicized experiments with school organization should facilitate change in the 1970's. The articulation between the college professor of English and his colleague in the junior college, the secondary school, or the elementary school which became a reality in this decade will become a commonplace in the next. Most important, the discipline of English, once the preserve of the Brahmin and the despair of the immigrant and the disadvantaged, will help to bring about the great social revolution now taking place in the United States. One can make no greater claim for the relevance of English to American life.

Notes

Chapter I—The English Curriculum

[1]James E. Miller, Jr., "Literature in the Revitalized Curriculum," *NASSP Bulletin*, Vol. 51, No. 318 (April 1967), pp. 25–29. The entire issue of the *Bulletin* was devoted to "The English Curriculum in the Secondary School."

[2]Irving Gersten, "Introduction and Summation" to James J. Lynch and Bertrand Evans, *High School English Textbooks* (New York, 1963), pp. 5–7; see also p. 242.

[3]*The Basic Issues in the Teaching of English* (New York, 1959), pp. 6 ff., first published in *PMLA* Vol. LXXIV, No. 4, Part 2 (September 1959), pp. 1–12.

[4]*Freedom and Discipline in English: Report of the Commission on English* (New York, 1965), p. 2.

[5]Harold B. Allen, "The 'New English' Anew," *NASSP Bulletin*, Vol. 51, No. 318 (April 1967), p. 18. See also "Trends in Teaching Language," *The Future of the English Curriculum*, ed. James D. Barry (New York, 1967), p. 13.

[6]Jerome Bruner, *The Process of Education* (New York, 1963, Copyright, 1960, by the President and Fellows of Harvard College), pp. 6 ff.

[7]G. Robert Carlsen and James Crow, "Project English Curriculum Centers," *English Journal*, Vol. 56, No. 7 (October 1967), p. 993.

[8]Miller, p. 20.

[9]Northrop Frye, "Elementary Teaching and Elementary Scholarship," *PMLA*, Vol. LXXIX, No. 2 (May 1964), pp. 11, 13, 14.

[10]Marjorie Smiley, "Research and Its Implications," *Improving English Skills of Culturally Different Youth* (Washington, 1964), pp. 35, 55.

[11]Richard Corbin, Muriel Crosby, and the NCTE Task Force on Teaching English to the Disadvantaged, *Language Programs for the Disadvantaged* (Champaign, Ill., 1965), pp. v, 271 ff.

[12]Ralph C. M. Flynt, "The U.S. Office of Education Looks at Project English," *PMLA,* Vol. LXXVIII, No. 4, Part 2 (September 1963), pp. 30, 31, 32.

[13]J. N. Hook, "Project English: The First Year," *PMLA,* Vol. LXXVIII, No. 4, Part 2 (September 1963), pp. 33–34.

[14]Erwin R. Steinberg, *Needed Research in the Teaching of English* (Washington, 1963), p. 128. See also "Research on the Teaching of English Under Project English," *PMLA,* Vol. LXXIX, No. 4, Part 2 (September 1964), pp. 50–76, and Robert C. Slack, "A Report on Project English," *English Journal,* Vol. 53, No. 9 (December 1964), pp. 681–686.

[15]Robert W. Rogers, "Opening Remarks," *Proceedings of the Allerton Park Conference on Research in the Teaching of English* (Urbana, Ill., 1963), p. 4.

[16]Robert W. Rogers, "A Dean Speaks Out," *ADE Bulletin* (October 1967), pp. 14–15.

[17]See Michael Shugrue, Carl Barth, and Leo Ruth, *An Evaluation of the Use of English Institute Materials Center Curriculum Materials in NDEA Summer Institutes in English* (New York, 1966) and James D. Barry, ed. *The Future of the English Curriculum* (New York, 1967). See also the report by Donald J. Gray entitled *The 1965 Institutes in English* (New York, 1966).

[18]Carlsen, pp. 986, 990, 992.

[19]Albert R. Kitzhaber, "The Government and English Teaching: A Retrospective View," *College Composition and Communication* (October 1967), pp. 139–141.

[20]Robert Shafer, "Curriculum: New Perspectives," *English Journal,* Vol. 56, No. 1 (January 1967), pp. 151, 160.

[21]Herbert J. Muller, *The Uses of English* (New York, 1967), pp. 50, 51, 54.

[22]Wayne C. Booth, "The Undergraduate Program," *The College Teaching of English,* ed. John C. Gerber (New York, 1965), p. 221. See also Thomas Wilcox, "The Study of Undergraduate English Programs: Some Preliminary Findings," *College English,* Vol. 29, No. 6 (March 1968), pp. 440–449.

[23]Hoyt Trowbridge, "Introductory Literature Courses," *The College Teaching of English,* p. 42.

[24]Robert M. Gorrell, "Freshman Composition," *The College Teaching of English,* p. 100. The definitive study of freshman composition is Albert C. Kitzhaber's *Themes, Theories, and Therapy* (New York, 1963).

[25]Michael Shugrue, "New Materials for the Teaching of English," *PMLA,* Vol. LXXXI, No. 4 (September 1966), p. 23.

[26]Paul Olson, "Introduction: The Drift of the Conference," *The Arts of Language* (Lincoln, Nebraska, 1966), pp. 8, 10, 19.

[27]See the report on *The Tri-University Project in Elementary Education* issued by the Office of Education on July 5, 1967, pp. 4–5.

[28]My thanks to Professors Dudley Bailey and Frank M. Rice for compiling these statistics.

[29]"New Materials for the Teaching of English," pp. 3–7. See "The Overall Plan" in *A Senior High School Curriculum in English for Able College-Bound Students,* pp. 1–12

and 'The Inductive Teaching of English," pp. 13, 15, 21. Barnes and Noble began to publish the Carnegie materials in 1968.

³⁰ "A Curriculum in English—Grades 7-12," prepared by the Curriculum Study Center in English at the University of Oregon and distributed to NDEA Institutes through the English Institute Materials Center in 1966 and 1967, pp. i ff. Holt, Rinehart and Winston began to publish the Oregon materials in 1968.

³¹See Donald R. Bateman and Frank J. Zidonis, *The Effect of a Study of Transformational Grammar on the Writing of Ninth and Tenth Graders* (Champaign, Ill., 1966).

³²*Teacher's Manual* to *Gateway English* (New York, 1966), pp. 1 ff. The Macmillan Company began to publish the Gateway materials in 1966.

³³See Daniel N. Fader and Elton B. McNeil, *Hooked on Books: Program and Proof* (New York, 1968), pp. 16, 17.

³⁴"Introduction" to *Lessons in Composition for High Schools* prepared by the Northwestern Curriculum Study Center in English and distributed to NDEA Institutes in 1967, pp. 2 ff.

³⁵See Albert H. Marckwardt, "The Dartmouth Seminar," *NASSP Bulletin*, Vol. 51, No. 318 (April 1967), pp. 104-105.

³⁶Muller, pp. vi ff.

³⁷John Dixon, "Author's Preface" to *Growth through English* (Reading, 1967), p. xi.

³⁸Wallace W. Douglas, "English: One Road or Many? Some Historical Reflections," Working Paper III at Dartmouth.

³⁹Arthur Eastman, "Trends in Teaching Literature," *The Future of the English Curriculum*, ed. James D. Barry (New York, 1967), p. 4.

⁴⁰William Arrowsmith, "The Future of Teaching," *Improving College Teaching*, ed. Calvin B. T. Lee (Washington, 1967), p. 64.

⁴¹Martin Trow, "Undergraduate Teaching at Large State Universities," *Improving College Teaching*, p. 173.

⁴²See Samuel Baskin, "Innovation in College Teaching," *Improving College Teaching*, pp. 181-196.

⁴³John C. Gerber, "The Chairman and His Department," *ADE Bulletin* (October 1967), p. 7.

Chapter II—The Teacher of English

¹See also James F. Rogers *Staffing American Colleges and Universities* (Washington, D.C., 1967), p. 9. *Projections of Educational Statistics to 1975-1976*, published by the National Center for Educational Statistics (Washington, 1966) and "The Magnitude of the American Educational Establishment 1967-1968," *Saturday Review* (21 October 1967), p. 67.

²*The National Interest and the Continuing Education of Teachers of English* (Champaign, Ill., 1964), p. 4.

³Clifford F. S. Bebell, *Designing Education for the Future* (Denver, 1967), p. 22.

⁴Jacques Barzun, *The Teacher in America* (New York, 1954, orig. publ. 1944), p. 262.

[5]Don Cameron Allen, *The Ph.D. in English and American Literature* (New York, 1968), Table 7.20 ff.

[6]Addressing the first Plenary Session of the MLA in New York City on 30 March 1967.

[7]Frank G. Jennings, "The Revolution in Education: It Didn't Start with Sputnik," *Saturday Review* (September 16, 1967), pp. 77 ff.

[8]*The National Interest and the Teaching of English* (Champaign, Ill., 1961), pp. 33, 39–42.

[9]G. K. Hodenfield and T. M. Stinnett, *The Education of Teachers* (Englewood Cliffs, N.J., 1961), p. 69.

[10]James D. Koerner, *The Miseducation of American Teachers* (Boston, 1963), pp. 263–264.

[11]Harold W. Dodds, *The Academic President: Educator or Caretaker* (New York, 1962), p. 118; Charles Muscatine, "The Role of the University in Society," *Duke Alumni Register* (June 1967), p. 22.

[12]James B. Conant, *The American High School Today* (New York, 1959), pp. 23, 47, 50–51, 55. In *The Comprehensive High School* (1967), Conant concluded that "in all probability courses in English composition are far better staffed than was the case 10 years ago, but many schools still have too few English teachers" (p. 39).

[13]James R. Squire, ed. *High School Departments of English: Their Organization, Administration, and Supervision* (Champaign, Ill., 1964), pp. 26–28. The report was based on two national conferences supported by the Cooperative Research Program of the USOE. See also Squire's monumental *A Study of English Programs in Selected High Schools Which Consistently Educate Outstanding Students in English* (1966) and *A Study of the Teaching of English in Selected British Secondary Schools* (1968).

[14]Eldonna L. Evertts, "Literature and Composition in the Elementary Grades," *New Directions in Elementary Education*, ed. Alexander Frazier (Champaign, Ill., 1967), p. 207.

[15]*Freedom and Discipline in English*, pp. 1, 5, 7, 10–11.

[16]Wallace W. Douglas, "Essay Review: *Freedom and Discipline in English*," *The School Review*, Vol. 75, No. 2 (Summer 1967), p. 227; *Ends and Issues*, ed. Alexander Frazier (Champaign, Ill., 1966), pp. 1, 39.

[17]John C. Gerber, "The 1962 Summer Institutes of the Commission on English: Their Achievement and Promise," *PMLA*, Vol. LXXVIII, No. 4, Part 2 (September 1963), p. 9. See also his *The Evaluation of the 1962 English Institutes* (New York, 1964).

[18]*The Education of Teachers of English for American Schools and Colleges*, ed. Alfred H. Grommon for the NCTE Commission on the English Curriculum (New York, 1963), pp. 4 ff.

[19]*PMLA*, Vol. LXXX, No. 4, Part 2 (September 1965), p. A-16.

[20]Bernard Berelson, *Graduate Education in the United States* (New York, 1960), pp. 234 ff.

[21]Allen, pp. 109 ff.

[22]*PMLA*, Vol. LXXXII, No. 4 (September 1967), pp. A-10–11.

[23]Frank Whitehead, *The Disappearing Dais* (London, 1966), pp. 16, 17, 21.

24David Holbrook, *English for the Rejected* (Cambridge, 1964), pp. 192, 199, 206–208.

25Working papers of the Dartmouth Conference, XVI, 27–28.

26See *The Final Report of the Minnesota Colleges Conferences on English Teacher Preparation. Issues in the Preparation of Teachers of English*, ed. Raymond D. Crisp (Urbana, 1967), describes many of the research projects undertaken by ISCPET colleges.

27Reprints of the *Guidelines* are available from NCTE and from MLA.

28The Scholar's Book Club, established by the MLA in 1967, has demonstrated that college professors of English and the modern foreign languages are beginning to purchase larger numbers of scholarly books published by the university presses.

29Paul Goodman, "The Role of the Individual in the University," *Duke Alumni Register* (June 1967), p. 12.

30Muscatine, p. 20.

31David A. Goslin, "What's Wrong with Tests and Testing," *College Board Review*, Nos. 65 and 66 (Fall and Winter 1967), pp. 13 ff. See his *Search for Ability* (New York, 1963).

32Roald F. Campbell, "Tomorrow's Teacher," *Saturday Review* (January 14, 1967), p. 63.

33Edmund J. Farrell, *English, Education, and the Electronic Revolution* (Champaign, Ill., 1967), p. 51.

34William G. Harley, "Techniques and Costs," *Saturday Review* (January 14, 1967), p. 54.

35Jack Nelson and Gene Roberts, Jr., *The Censors and the Schools* (Boston, 1963), p. 182.

36*The Students' Right to Read* (Champaign, Ill., 1962), pp. 1–21.

37Albert H. Kitzhaber, "English Instruction in Two-Year Colleges: Problems and Possibilities," *Research and the Development of English Programs in the Junior College*, ed. Jerome W. Archer (Champaign, Ill., 1965), pp. 5–6.

38H. K. Newburn, "Comments on *English in the Two-Year College*," *Research and the Development of English Programs in the Junior College*, p. 36.

39Roger H. Garrison, *Junior College Faculty: Issues and Problems* (Washington, 1967), pp. 40, 72, 74.

40See Samuel Weingarten and Frederick Kroeger, *English in the Two-Year College* (Champaign, Ill., 1965).

41Quoting Benjamin DeMott in *The Future of the English Curriculum*, p. 7; Daniel Bell, *The Reforming of General Education* (New York, 1966), p. 124.

Chapter III—English, Education, and Change

1See *College English*, Vol. 28, No. 1 (October 1966), pp. 55–57.

2Thomas Wilcox, "Teaching Loads," *ADE Bulletin* (February 1968), p. 4.

3*Ibid.*, p. 5.

[4]William Buckler, "Teaching Loads—and Other Myths," *ADE Bulletin* (February 1968), p. 7.

[5]John Goodlad, *The Changing School Curriculum* (New York, 1966), pp. 15, 17, 111.

[6]John Maxwell, "Readiness for New Curriculum Materials," *English Journal,* Vol. 56, No. 9 (December 1967), pp. 1338–1341.

[7]Nat Hentoff, "Youth—The Oppressed Majority," *Playboy* (September 1967), p. 188.

[8]Arrowsmith, p. 68.

[9]Alexander W. Astin and Calvin B. T. Lee, "Current Practices in the Evaluation and Training of College Teachers," *Improving College Teaching,* ed. Calvin B. T. Lee (Washington, 1967), p. 298.

[10]Donald D. O'Dowd, "Closing the Gap," *Improving College Teaching,* p. 249.

[11]W. Max Wise, "Who Teaches the Teachers?", *Improving College Teaching,* pp. 80, 83.

[12]Allan M. Cartter, "University Teaching and Excellence," *Improving College Teaching,* p. 162.

[13]Robert W. Rogers, "The Department of English: Organization and Administration," *The College Teaching of English,* p. 296.

[14]James Boswell, *The Life of Dr. Johnson* (London, 1957), pp. 356, 1136.

[15]Joseph Axelrod, *New Patterns in Undergraduate Education: Emerging Curriculum Models for the American College,* No. 15 of *New Dimensions in Higher Education* (April 1967), pp. 4 ff. See also Cartter and Baskin in *Improving College Teaching.*

[16]Harold C. Martin, "A College President Speaks Out," *ADE Bulletin* (October 1967), pp. 18–22.

[17]Farrell, p. 10.

[18]Richard Scowcroft, "Courses in Creative Writing," *The College Teaching of English,* pp. 148–149.

[19]*Ibid.,* p. 149.

[20]Reed Whittemore, *The Writer on Campus,* working paper for the MLA-American Center of P.E.N. Conference on the Role of the Writer on Campus, February 12, 1968, pp. 28, 31.

[21]Farrell, p. 13.

[22]Peter Schrag, "Kids, Computers, and Corporations," *Saturday Review* (May 20, 1967), pp. 78, 79, 80, 96.

[23]Those who cannot visit the Brentwood School in Palo Alto can read Donald Suppes, "The Computer and Excellence," *Saturday Review* (January 14, 1967), pp. 46–50.

[24]Tom Phillips, "Beatles 'Sgt. Pepper': The Album as Art Form," *The Village Voice* (June 22, 1967), p. 15.

[25]John M. Culkin, S.J., "The Name of the Game Is Excitement," *New York Times* (July 2, 1967), Section 2, p. 11.

[26]As quoted in Charles and Bonnie Remsberg, "Chicago: Legacy of an Ice Age," *Saturday Review* (May 20, 1967), p. 73.

[27]*Ibid.*, p. 74.

[28]See, for example, the inventories of *Projects and Activities in Reading and English*, published by the Center for Applied Linguistics.

[29]James R. Squire, "Preface" to *Obscenity, the Law, and the English Teacher* (Champaign, Ill., 1966).

[30]Robert F. Hogan, "Obscenity and the Teacher: Another View," *Obscenity, the Law, and the English Teacher*, pp. 60, 61.

[31]Hillel Black, *The Truth About College Entrance Exams and Other Standardized Tests* (New York, 1963), pp. 166, 255. See also Banesh Hoffman, *The Tyranny of Testing* (New York, 1962).

[32]Goslin, *The Search for Ability*, p. 156.

List of Works Cited

Allen, Don Cameron. *The Ph.D. in English and American Literature.* New York, 1968.

Allen, Harold B. "The 'New English' Anew," *NASSP Bulletin,* Number 318, April 1967.

The Arts of Language: Needed Curricula and Curriculum Development for Institutes in the English Language Arts, ed. Paul A. Olson. 1966.

Axelrod, Joseph. *New Patterns in Undergraduate Education: Emerging Curriculum Models for the American College,* Number 15 of *New Dimensions in Higher Education.* April 1967.

Barzun, Jacques. *The Teacher in America.* New York, 1954, originally published 1944.

The Basic Issues in the Teaching of English. New York, 1959.

Bateman, Donald R. and Frank J. Zidonis. *The Effect of a Study of Transformational Grammar on the Writing of Ninth and Tenth Graders.* Champaign, Illinois, 1966.

Bebell, Clifford F. S. *Designing Education for the Future.* Denver, Colorado, 1967.

Bell, Daniel. *The Reforming of General Education.* New York, 1966.

Berelson, Bernard. *Graduate Education in the United States.* New York, 1960.

Black, Hillel. *The Truth About College Entrance Exams and Other Standardized Tests.* New York, 1963.

Bruner, Jerome. *The Process of Education.* New York, 1963, originally published 1960.

Buckler, William. "Teaching Loads—and Other Myths," *ADE Bulletin,* February 1968.

Campbell, Roald F. "Tomorrow's Teacher," *Saturday Review,* January 14, 1967.

Carlsen, G. Robert and James Crow. "Project English Curriculum Centers," *English Journal,* Volume 56, Number 7, October 1967.

The College Teaching of English, ed. John C. Gerber. New York, 1965.

Conant, James B. *The American High School Today.* New York, 1959.

Conant, James B. *The Comprehensive High School.* New York, 1967.

Corbin, Richard and Muriel Crosby. *Language Programs for the Disadvantaged.* Champaign, Illinois, 1965.

Culkin, John M., S.J. "The Name of the Game Is Excitement," *New York Times,* July 2, 1967.

"A Curriculum in English—Grades 7-12," prepared by the Curriculum Study Center in English at the University of Oregon, 1966 and 1967.

Dixon, John. *Growth through English.* Reading, England, 1967.

Dodds, Harold W. *The Academic President: Educator or Caretaker.* New York, 1962.

Eble, Kenneth. *The Profane Comedy: American Higher Education in the Sixties.* New York, 1962.

The Education of Teachers of English for American Schools and Colleges, ed. Alfred H. Grommon. New York, 1963.

Ends and Issues, ed. Alexander Frazier. Champaign, Illinois, 1966.

Fader, Daniel N. and Elton B. McNeil. *Hooked on Books: Program and Proof.* New York, 1968.

Farrell, Edmund J. *English, Education, and the Electronic Revolution.* Champaign, Illinois, 1967.

Flynt, Ralph C. M. "The U. S. Office of Education looks at Project English," *PMLA,* Volume LXXVIII, Number 4, Part 2, September 1963.

Freedom and Discipline in English: Report of the Commission on English. New York, 1965.

Frye, Northrop. "Elementary Teaching and Elementary Scholarship," *PMLA,* Volume LXXIX, Number 2, May 1964.

The Future of the English Curriculum, ed. James D. Barry. New York, 1967.

Garrison, Roger H. *Junior College Faculty: Issues and Problems.* Washington, 1967.

Gateway English. New York, 1966 and following.

Gerber, John C. "The Chairman and His Department," *ADE Bulletin,* October 1967.

Gerber, John C. *The Evaluation of the 1962 English Institutes.* New York, 1964.

Gerber, John C. "The 1962 Summer Institutes of the Commission on English: Their Achievement and Promise," *PMLA,* Volume LXXVIII, Number 4, Part 2, September 1963.

Goodlad, John. *The Changing School Curriculum.* New York, 1966.

Goodman, Paul. "The Role of the Individual in the University," *Duke Alumni Register,* June 1967.

Goslin, David A. *The Search for Ability.* New York, 1963.

Goslin, David A. "What's Wrong with Tests and Testing," *College Board Review,* Numbers 65 and 66, Fall and Winter 1967.

Gray, Donald J. *The 1965 Institutes in English.* New York, 1966.

Grommon, Alfred H. "A History of the Preparation of Teachers of English," *English Journal,* Volume 57, Number 4, April 1968.

Guidelines for the Preparation of Teachers of English—An Exposition. Champaign, Illinois, and New York, 1968.

Harley, William G. "Techniques and Costs," *Saturday Review,* January 14, 1967.

Hentoff, Nat. "Youth—The Oppressed Majority," *Playboy,* September 1967.

Hodenfield, G. K. and T. M. Stinnett. *The Education of Teachers.* Englewood Cliffs, New Jersey, 1961.

Hoffman, Banesh. *The Tyranny of Testing.* New York, 1962.

Holbrook, David. *English for the Rejected.* Cambridge, England, 1964.

Hook, J. N. "Project English: The First Year," *PMLA,* Volume LXXVIII, Number 4, Part 2, September 1963.

Improving College Teaching, ed. Calvin B. T. Lee. Washington, 1967.

Issues in the Preparation of Teachers of English, ed. Raymond D. Crisp. Urbana, Illinois, 1967.

Jennings, Frank G. "The Revolution in Education: It Didn't Start with Sputnik," *Saturday Review,* September 16, 1967.

Kitzhaber, Albert R. "The Government and English Teaching: A Retrospective View," *College Composition and Communication,* October 1967.

Kitzhaber, Albert R. *Themes, Theories, and Therapy.* New York, 1963.

Koerner, James D. *The Miseducation of American Teachers.* Boston, Massachusetts, 1963.

Lessons in Composition for High Schools prepared by the Northwestern Curriculum Study Center in English, 1967.

Lynch, James J. and Bertrand Evans. *High School English Textbooks.* New York, 1963.

Marckwardt, Albert H. "The Dartmouth Seminar," *NASSP Bulletin,* Number 318, April 1967.

Martin, Harold C. "A College President Speaks Out," *ADE Bulletin,* October 1967.

Maxwell, John. "Readiness for New Curriculum Materials," *English Journal,* Volume 56, Number 9, December 1967.

Miller, James E., Jr. "Literature in the Revitalized Curriculum," *NASSP Bulletin,* Number 318, April 1967.

Muller, Herbert J. *The Uses of English*. New York, 1967.

Muscatine, Charles. "The Role of the University in Society," *Duke Alumni Register*, June 1967.

The National Interest and the Teaching of English. Champaign, Illinois, 1961.

The National Interest and the Continuing Education of Teachers of English. Champaign, Illinois, 1964.

The Nebraska Curriculum for English. Lincoln, Nebraska, 1967.

Nelson, Jack and Gene Roberts, Jr. *The Censors and the Schools*. Boston, Massachusetts, 1963.

New Directions in Elementary Education, ed. Alexander Frazier. Champaign, Illinois, 1967.

Obscenity, the Law, and the English Teacher. Champaign, Illinois, 1966.

Phillips, Tom. "Beatles 'Sgt. Pepper': The Album as Art Form," *The Village Voice*, June 22, 1967.

Proceedings of the Allerton Park Conference on Research in the Teaching of English, ed. Robert W. Rogers. Urbana, Illinois, 1963.

Projections of Educational Statistics to 1975-1976. Washington, 1966.

Projects and Activities in Reading and English. Washington, 1967 and following.

Remsberg, Charles and Bonnie, "Chicago: Legacy of an Ice Age," *Saturday Review*, May 20, 1967.

Research and the Development of English Programs in the Junior College, ed. Jerome W. Archer. Champaign, Illinois, 1965.

Rogers, James F., *Staffing American Colleges and Universities*. Washington, D.C., 1967.

Rogers, Robert W. "A Dean Speaks Out," *ADE Bulletin*, October 1967.

Schrag, Peter. "Kids, Computers, and Corporations," *Saturday Review*, May 20, 1967.

A Senior High School Curriculum in English for Able College-Bound Students. Pittsburgh, Pennsylvania, 1967.

Shugrue, Michael F. and Thomas F. Crawley, "The Conclusion of the Initial Phase: The English Program of the USOE," *PMLA*, Volume LXXXII, Number 4, September 1967.

Shugrue, Michael F., Carl A. Barth, and Leo Ruth. *An Evaluation of the Use of English Institute Materials Center Curriculum Materials in NDEA Summer Institutes in English*. New York, 1966.

Shugrue, Michael F. "New Materials for the Teaching of English: The English Program of the USOE," *PMLA*, Volume LXXXI, Number 4, September 1966.

Slack, Robert C. "A Report on Project English," *English Journal*, Volume 53, Number 9, December 1964.

Squire, James R. *High School Departments of English: Their Organization, Administration, and Supervision.* Champaign, Illinois, 1964.

Squire, James R. *A Study of English Programs in Selected High Schools Which Consistently Educate Outstanding Students in English.* USOE Cooperative Research Project, Number 1994, Urbana, Illinois, 1966.

Squire, James R. *A Study of the Teaching of English in Selected British Secondary Schools.* USOE Cooperative Research Project, Number 61849, Washington, 1968.

Steinberg, Erwin R. *Needed Research in the Teaching of English.* Washington, 1963.

Steinberg, Erwin R. "Research on the Teaching of English Under Project English," *PMLA*, Volume LXXIX, Number 4, Part 2, September 1964.

The Students' Right to Read. Champaign, Illinois, 1962.

Suppes, Donald. "The Computer and Excellence," *Saturday Review*, 14 January 1967.

Weingarten, Samuel and Frederick Kroeger: *English in the Two-Year College.* Champaign, Illinois, 1965.

Whitehead, Frank. *The Disappearing Dais.* London, 1966.

Wilcox, Thomas. "The Study of Undergraduate English Programs: Some Preliminary Findings," *College English*, Volume 29, Number 6, March 1968.

Wilcox, Thomas. "Teaching Loads," *ADE Bulletin*, February 1968.

Working Papers of the Anglo-American Conference on the Teaching of English. 2 volumes.

Index